First World War
and Army of Occupation
War Diary
France, Belgium and Germany

36 DIVISION
Divisional Troops
Divisional Signal Company
2 October 1915 - 31 January 1919

WO95/2498/1

The Naval & Military Press Ltd
www.nmarchive.com
Published in association with The National Archives

Published by

The Naval & Military Press Ltd

Unit 10 Ridgewood Industrial Park,

Uckfield, East Sussex,

TN22 5QE England

Tel: +44 (0) 1825 749494

www.naval-military-press.com

www.nmarchive.com

This diary has been reprinted in facsimile from the original. Any imperfections are inevitably reproduced and the quality may fall short of modern type and cartographic standards.

© Crown Copyright
Images reproduced by permission of The National Archives, London, England, 2015.

Contents

Document type	Place/Title	Date From	Date To
Heading	WO95/2498/1 36th Divisional Signal Company		
Heading	36th Divl. Signals Coy. Vol I Oct 15		
Heading	War Diary Of 36th Divisional Signal Company, Royal Engineers. From 2nd. Day Of October, 1915 To 31st Day Of October 1915. Volume I		
War Diary	Bordon.	02/10/1915	02/10/1915
War Diary	Havre	03/10/1915	03/10/1915
War Diary	Flesselles.	04/10/1915	18/10/1915
War Diary	Domart En Ponthieu.	22/10/1915	24/10/1915
War Diary	Flesselles.	19/10/1915	21/10/1915
War Diary	Domart En Ponthieu.	25/10/1915	31/10/1915
Map	Ref. Map.-Amiens-Sheet 12-1.80,000		
Heading	36th Div. Sig. Coy RE. Vol. 2 Nov 15		
Heading	War Diary Of 36th Divisional Signal Company, Royal Engineers. From, 1st November. 1915 To 1st November. 1915. Volume 2		
War Diary	Domart En Ponthieu.	01/11/1915	24/11/1915
War Diary	Domart En Ponthieu	25/11/1915	25/11/1915
War Diary	Domart En Ponthieu.	26/11/1915	28/11/1915
War Diary	Pont Remy.	29/11/1915	30/11/1915
Map	Communications 36th Signal Company.		
Heading	36th Div. Sig. Coy. RE. Vol 3		
Heading	War Diary Of 36th Divisional Signal Company R.E. From 1st December. 1915 To 31st December. 1915. Volume Three.		
War Diary	Pont Remy	01/12/1915	31/12/1915
Map	Communications 36th Signal Company R.E		
Heading	36th Div. Signals Vol 4		
Heading	War Diary Of 36th Divisional Signal Company, Royal Engineers. From 1st January, 1916 To 31st January. 1916 Volume Four.		
War Diary	Pont Remy.	01/01/1916	02/01/1916
War Diary	Domart En Ponthieu	03/01/1916	18/01/1916
War Diary	Bernaville	20/01/1916	31/01/1916
Map			
Diagram etc	Communications 36th Signal Company R.E.		
Diagram etc	Communications 30th Division. Sigs.		
Diagram etc	Circuit Diagram.		
Map	Scale 1.40.000		
Heading	36th Div Sig Co R.E. Vol 5		
War Diary	Bernaville	01/02/1916	06/02/1916
War Diary	Acheux	07/02/1916	29/02/1916
Diagram etc	Telegraph Circuits. 36th Div. Sig. Coy. R.E Appendice "A"		
Diagram etc	Telephone System-36th Division.		
Diagram etc	Circuit Diagram Appendice B		
Heading	War Diary Of 36th Divisional Signal Company, R.E From 1st March, 1916 To 31st March. 1916 Volume Six		
War Diary	Acheux	01/03/1916	31/03/1916

Heading	War Diary Of 36th Divisional Signal Company. R.E. From 1st April, 1916 To 30th April 1916 Volume The Sixth.		
Miscellaneous	Officer 1/0 Adjutant General's Office. at the Base. Vol 7	03/06/1916	03/06/1916
War Diary	Acheux	01/04/1916	03/04/1916
War Diary	Harponville.	04/04/1916	20/04/1916
War Diary	Hedauville	21/04/1916	30/04/1916
Heading	War Diary Of 36th Divisional Signal Company, R.E From 1st May, 1916 To 31st May, 1916 Volume The Eight.		
Miscellaneous	Officer i/c Adjutant General's Office, Base. Vol 8	06/06/1916	06/06/1916
War Diary	Hedauville	01/05/1916	31/05/1916
Heading	36th Divisional Engineers 36th Divisional Signal Company R.E. June 1916		
Miscellaneous	D.A.G. 3rd Echelon. Vol 9	09/07/1916	09/07/1916
War Diary	In The Field.	01/06/1916	30/06/1916
Heading	36th Divisional Engineers 36th Divisional Signal Company July 1916		
War Diary	In The Field.	01/08/1916	11/08/1916
War Diary	In The Field	01/07/1916	28/02/1918
Heading	36th Divisional Engineers 36th Divisional Signal Company R.E. March 1918		
War Diary	Ollezy	01/03/1918	21/03/1918
War Diary	Estouilly	22/03/1918	31/03/1918
Heading	36th Divisional Engineers 36th Divisional Signal Company R.E. April 1918.		
War Diary	Gamaches	01/04/1918	04/04/1918
War Diary	Poperinghe	05/04/1918	07/04/1918
War Diary	Canal Bank.	08/04/1918	21/04/1918
War Diary	Border Camp	22/04/1918	22/04/1918
War Diary	Poperinghe	23/04/1918	30/04/1918
War Diary	In The Field	01/05/1918	30/06/1918
War Diary	Pardo Camp (Proven)	01/07/1918	03/07/1918
War Diary	Cassel	04/07/1918	07/07/1918
War Diary	Mont-Des-Cats.	08/07/1918	14/07/1918
War Diary	Terdeghem	15/07/1918	31/07/1918
War Diary		01/09/1918	30/09/1918
War Diary		01/10/1918	31/10/1918
War Diary	Belleghem	29/10/1918	03/11/1918
War Diary	Mouscron	04/11/1918	31/01/1919

WO95/2498/1
36th Divisional Signal Company

12/7432

36th Divis[ion]

36th Divl: Sigd Coy:
vol I

Oct 15

Confidential

WAR – DIARY

~ OF ~

36th DIVISIONAL SIGNAL COMPANY, ROYAL ENGINEERS.

From.

2ND. DAY OF OCTOBER, 1915 — To — 31ST day of OCTOBER, 1915

VOLUME — ONE

36th (Ulster) Div. Signal Coy R.E.

Army Form C. 2118.

WAR DIARY
or
INTELLIGENCE SUMMARY.
(Erase heading not required.)

Instructions regarding War Diaries and Intelligence Summaries are contained in F.S. Regs., Part II. and the Staff Manual respectively. Title pages will be prepared in manuscript.

Place	Date	Hour	Summary of Events and Information	Remarks and references to Appendices
BORDON.	2:x:15		H.Q. and No. 1 and 2 Section entrained at BORDON for SOUTHAMPTON and embarked same evening for FRANCE.	
HAVRE	3:x:15		H.Q. and No 1 Section arrived HAVRE and entrained same evening - No 2 Section also disembarked at HAVRE.	
			No 3 Section embarked at SOUTHAMPTON for HAVRE.	
FLESSELLES	4:x:15		H.Q., No 1 and 2 Sections, detrained at LONGUEAU and marched to FLESSELLES, No 2 Section proceeding to VIGNACOURT, at which places Signal Offices were established. No 3 Section disembarked at HAVRE and entrained the same evening. No 4 Section entrained at LIPHOOK and detrained at SOUTHAMPTON, embarking same evening for FRANCE.	
FLESSELLES	5:x:15		H.Q. and No 1 Section. Communication to H.Q. VII Corps, 107th and 109th Bdes. using spare permanent lines, and Cable. Signal Office opened at 10 a.m.	
			No 2 Section. Signal Office opened at 11 a.m. At 4.15 p.m. line changed onto Permanent line.	
			No 3 Section. Detrained at LONGUEAU and marched to MOLLIENS aux BOIS. Office opened here at 5 p.m.	
			Cable Wagon arrived and communication opened up with FLESSELLES.	
			No 4 Section. Disembarked at HAVRE, entrained same night.	
FLESSELLES	6:x:15		A good deal of induction on the lines.	
			No 2 Section - Communication to Bde. by D.R.s. 8th R.I.R. at ST VAAST - 9th, 10th and 15th R.I.R. at VIGNACOURT.	
			No 3 Section. Lines laid to Bns as follows :- 11th, 12th, 13th, R. Ir. Rif. at RUBEMPRE, PIERREGOT, and RAINNEVILLE	

WAR DIARY or INTELLIGENCE SUMMARY

Army Form C. 2118.

36th (Ulster) Div. Signal Coy. R.E

Place	Date	Hour	Summary of Events and Information	Remarks and references to Appendices
FLESSELLES	7.X.15		RAINNEVILLE respectively	
			No 4 Section - Arrived LONGUEAU - marched to BERTANGLES.	
			H.Q. & No 1 Section. Communication satisfactory until 5.30 p.m. when owing to instructions orders received to remove lines from permanent poles. XX Cable Section attached to H.Q. Friday	
			No 2 Section - Cable laid to ST. VAST - Line broken on 2 occasions	
			No 3 Section - Communication Satisfactory	
			No 4 Section - Communication opened up with 109 Bde. H.Q., 10th R. Innis. Bn. at COISY, 11th R. Innis. Bn. at CARDONETTE and 14th R.I.R. at POULAINVILLE	
FLESSELLES	8.X.15		H.Q. & No 1 Section. Lines satisfactory	
			No 2 Section. Satisfactory. Speaking Telephone very faint to Bns. Orders from H.Q. 36th Div. to move tomorrow	
			No 3 Section - Communication satisfactory	
			No 4 Section - Communication to 9th R. Innis. Bn. opened by Cable at BERTANGLES.	
FLESSELLES	9.X.15		H.Q. & No 1 Section. Cable laid to replace lines used on permanent poles to XII Corps. Communication satisfactory	
			No 2 Section - Less 16 men marched from VIGNACOURT to HERISSART.	
			No 3 Section - Lines working satisfactorily	
			No 4 Section - Nothing to report. Communication satisfactory	

36th Signal Company R.E.

WAR DIARY
or
INTELLIGENCE SUMMARY.
(Erase heading not required.)

Army Form C. 2118.

Instructions regarding War Diaries and Intelligence Summaries are contained in F.S. Regs., Part II. and the Staff Manual respectively. Title pages will be prepared in manuscript.

Place	Date	Hour	Summary of Events and Information	Remarks and references to Appendices
FLESSELLES	10.X.15		H.Q. & No 1 Section. Lines satisfactory. XX Cable Section laid line from H.Q. Div. Arty. to Arty. Bdes.	
			No 2 Section - marched from HERISSART to ENGLEBELMER	
			No 3 Section. Communications on Buzzer good - Lamp Signalling opened with 11th R.Ir.Rif, 13th R.I.R. & 9th R.Ir.Fus at 4 p.m.	
			No 4 Section - Lines satisfactory	
FLESSELLES	11.X.15		Comic Air line FLESSELLES to MOLLIENS commenced to replace cable. Other lines satisfactory, except to No 3 Sec.	
			No 2 Section - Attached to the 4th Div in rear for instruction	
			No 3 Section. Visual Signalling opened with 11th R.I.R., 13th R.I.R. and 9th R.Ir.Fus - wire to H.Q. Sec. dis. at 6.40 p.m. through at 8.38 p.m. owing to a break.	
			No 4 Section - wires to 11th R.I.Fus. and 14th R.I.R. cut, and about 50 yds. of wire removed)	
FLESSELLES	12.X.15		H.Q. & No 1 Sec. Lines satisfactory. Working on Comic Air line to MOLLIENS.	
			No 2 Sec. Attached to 4th Div for instruction	
			No 3 Sec. Buzzer on line to 11th R.Ir.Rif. not working at 9.20 a.m. repaired 11 a.m. 13 R.I.R. moved to ST. GRATIEN line laid to him & communication opened at 5.30 p.m. Helio communication opened to 11th R.I.R., 13th R.I.R. & 9th R.Ir. Fus. at 3 p.m.	
			No 4 Section - Lines working satisfactorily	

Army Form C. 2118.

36th Signal Company R.E. WAR DIARY or INTELLIGENCE SUMMARY.

(Erase heading not required.)

Instructions regarding War Diaries and Intelligence Summaries are contained in F. S. Regs, Part II. and the Staff Manual respectively. Title pages will be prepared in manuscript.

Place	Date	Hour	Summary of Events and Information	Remarks and references to Appendices
FLESSELLES	13:X:15		H.Q. & No 1 Sec. Satisfactory - Continuing Corvie Air Line to MOLLIENS.	
			No 2 Sec. Attached 4th Div for Instruction	
			No 3 Sec. Communications satisfactory - 3 p.m. Helio signalling tested - 8 p.m. lamp signalling tested	
			No 4 Sec. All lines working well	
FLESSELLES	14:X:15		H.Q. & No 1 Sec. Communications satisfactory.	
			No 2 Sec. Attached 4th Div for Instruction	
			No 3 Sec. 2.12 p.m. Line to 9th R.I. 3rd Div. repaired 5 p.m. 6.30 p.m. Line to 13th R.I.R. broken in several places repaired at 9.20 p.m. Messages sent by lamp during time under repair. Other lines satisfactory.	
			No 4 Sec. Nothing to report. Communications good.	
FLESSELLES	15:X:15		H.Q. & No 1 Sec. Satisfactory.	
			No 2 Sec. Attached 4th Div for Instruction	
			No 3 Sec. Line to H.Q. Div. at 1.20 p.m. restored at 2.35 p.m. - 2.20 p.m. Line to 13th R.I.R. Dis. repaired 3 a.m. - 5.50 p.m. Lines to 11th R.I.R. and 13th R.I.R. dis. repaired at 7.5 p.m. and 7.25 p.m.	
			No 4 Sec. Lines satisfactory.	
FLESSELLES	16:X:15		H.Q. & No 1 Sec. Unusual Field day. Lines satisfactory	
			No 2 Sec. Attached 4th Div for Instruction.	

Army Form C. 2118.

36th Signal Company R.E. WAR DIARY or INTELLIGENCE SUMMARY.

(Erase heading not required.)

Instructions regarding War Diaries and Intelligence Summaries are contained in F. S. Regs., Part II. and the Staff Manual respectively. Title pages will be prepared in manuscript.

Place	Date	Hour	Summary of Events and Information	Remarks and references to Appendices
FLESSELLES	17.x.15		No 3 Sec. 6.35 a.m. line to 9th R.Ir.Ins.dis. Communication opened again at 11.40 a.m. - line to 13th R.I.R. dis. at 11.20 a.m. Repaired at 12.45 p.m. line to 11th R.I.R., 12th R.I.R. and 108 Fd Amb (all on one circuit) broken at 6.30 p.m. repaired at 8.30 pm. Communication worked by visual. No 4 Sec. Buzzer — Indicator Poling line to 10th R.I.Ins.Ins. Divisional Field day. H.Q. & No 1 Sec. During 15 induction line from Div. H.Q. to Rly. Station FLESSELLES removed from permanent poles and cable laid. Other lines satisfactory. Took over No 3 Sec. Office. No 2 Sec. left MARTINSART and marched to ENGLEBELMER. Billets here for the night No 3 Sec. Signal Offices at 13th R.I.R. and 9th R.Ir.Ins. closed down — lines rolled up. Signal Offices at 11th R.I.R. and 12th R.I.R. closed down at 12 noon. Relief from H.Q. of Sig. Coy. took over B.de. Offices. At 2.30 p.m. the Section marched to PUCHEVILLERS arriving here at 5 p.m. and went into billets. Communication was maintained by Cyclists No 4 Sec. Finished poling line to 10th R.Ir.Ins.Ins.	
FLESSELLES	18.x.15		H.Q. & No 1 Sec. lines working satisfactorily No 2 Sec. marched to HERISSART and went into billets No 3 Sec. left PUCHEVILLERS at 8.30 a.m., arrived COUIN at 1.20 p.m. Halted here for the night No 4 Sec. Poled line to 11th R.Irwin.Ins. at CARDONETTE, and 9th R.Irwin.Ins. at ALLONVILLE - line between 9th and	

1577 Wt.W10791/1773 500,000 1/15 D. D. & L. A.D.S.S./Forms/C. 2118.

Army Form C. 2118.

36th Signal Company R.E.

WAR DIARY
or
INTELLIGENCE SUMMARY.
(Erase heading not required.)

Place	Date	Hour	Summary of Events and Information	Remarks and references to Appendices
DOMART en PONTHIEU	22.X.15		No 3 Sec. attached 144th Bde. for instruction. No 4 Sec. - 1 a.m. All lines reeled up. 11.30 a.m. marched from BERTANGLES, arrived BEAUVAL at 4.30 p.m. H.Q. and No 1. Sec. Office closed and opened at DOMART en PONTHIEU at 12 noon. Permanent line utilized to VII Corps and III Army. No 2 Sec. Office closed - marched to ST. LEGER, arriving 4 p.m. No 3 Sec. attached 144th Bde. for instruction.	
			No 4 Sec. 11 a.m. Communication opened with H.Q. through BEAUVAL Telephone Exchange. 4.30 p.m. Communication established with 11th R.Luis. Bns. at CANDAS and 9th R.Luis. Bns. at FIENVILLERS - Air line belonging to III Army as far as CANDAS used.	
DOMART en PONTHIEU	23.X.15		H.Q. & No 1 Sec. D5 Cable laid to No 2 Sec. at ST LEGER, No 4 Sec. at BEAUVAL. Telephone communication established to Div. Train at MONTRELET. Communication to No 3 Sections through III Army Exchange. No 2 Sec. Communication to Bns. and other units by Despatch Riders. No 3 Sec. attached 144th Bde. for instruction. No 4 Sec. Communication with H.Q. established by direct line.	
DOMART en PONTHIEU	24.X.15		H.Q. & No 1 Sec. Telephone exchange set up. Communication between H.Q. Div. Arty and 1/4th London Bde. at BONNEVILLE, 1/2nd London Bde. R.F.A at BERNEUIL and 1/1st London Bde. at CANAPLES established by XX Cable Sec.	

Army Form C. 2118.

36th Signal Company R.E.   WAR DIARY or INTELLIGENCE SUMMARY.

Instructions regarding War Diaries and Intelligence Summaries are contained in F. S. Regs., Part II. and the Staff Manual respectively. Title pages will be prepared in manuscript.

(Erase heading not required.)

Place	Date	Hour	Summary of Events and Information	Remarks and references to Appendices
FLESSELLES	19:X:15		9th and 11th R. Irish. Ins. Cat.	
			H.Q. & No 1 Sec. All lines satisfactory.	
			No 2 Sec. marched to VIGNACOURT. Took over Bde. Office from H.Q. Sec. and opened up communication with units.	
			No 3 Sec. marched from COUIN, arrived HEBUTERNE at 4.30 p.m. and hall'd lines. Attached 144th Bde. for instruction. At 5 p.m. 3 men sent to each Bn. in Trenches.	
			No 4 Sec. Communications good – nothing to report.	
FLESSELLES	20:X:15		H.Q. & No 1. Sec. Comic Air line to No 3 Sec. at MOLLIENS aux BOIS completed. Telephone line to No 2 See at VIGNACOURT today disconnected from 12 noon to 3 p.m. on 21st. All work done on trusses. Communication to A.S.C. at BERTANGLES GAP near GAP maintained by cyclist.	
			Established by using existing permanent line and cable.	
			No 2 Sec. lines to 9th, 10th and 15th R.I.R. reeled up and communication maintained by cyclist.	
			No 3 Sec. Attached 144th Bde. for instruction.	
			No 4 Sec. Communications working satisfactorily.	
FLESSELLES	21:X:15		H.Q. & No 1 Sec. Owing to Div. moving to another area, all lines to 3 and 4 Secs. reeled up. Also line to 15 1/2 howitzer Bde. R.F.A.	
			No 2 Sec. Bivouaat Tactical Exercise.	

36th Signal Coy. R.E.

Army Form C. 2118.

WAR DIARY
or
INTELLIGENCE SUMMARY.
(Erase heading not required.)

Place	Date	Hour	Summary of Events and Information	Remarks and references to Appendices
DOMART en PONTHIEU	25:X:15		No 2 Sec. lines laid out to 8th, 10th and 15th Bns. R.I.R. No 3 Sec. attached 144th Bde. for instruction No 4 Sec. Communications satisfactory. H.Q. & No 1 Sec. Communications satisfactory - 109th Bde. with No 4 Sec. moved to VII Corps for Training. Relief from H.Q. are sent out to take over Office. Line to 109th Bde. dis from 6 to 7.30 p.m. No 2 Sec. Poled all lines to Bns No 3 Sec. Section marched from HEBUTERNE to COVIN, arriving 1.30 p.m. Halted here for night. No 4 Sec. Reeled up lines from CANDAS to BONNEVILLE and FIENVILLE R.S. Handed over Office to Relief from H.Q. marched to PUCHEVILLERS and halted here	
DOMART en PONTHIEU	26:X:15		H.Q. & No 1 Sec. Cable D/S laid to No 3 Sec. at RIBEAUCOURT. At 7 a.m. instrument fully - dis for 15 minutes No 2 Sec. Communications satisfactory. No 3 Sec. - At 9.45 a.m Section marched from COVIN to BEAUVAL, arriving 7.30 p.m. Halted for night No 4 Sec. moved to MAILLY-MAILLET. Attached to 12th Infy. Bde.	
DOMART en PONTHIEU	27:X:15		H.Q. & No 1 Sec. Line to III Army dis. from 7.15 a.m. to 10.30 a.m. Communication to No 3 Sec (108th Bde) opened at RIBEAUCOURT	

36th Signal Co. R.E.

Army Form C. 2118.

WAR DIARY
or
INTELLIGENCE SUMMARY.
(Erase heading not required.)

Instructions regarding War Diaries and Intelligence Summaries are contained in F. S. Regs., Part II. and the Staff Manual respectively. Title pages will be prepared in manuscript.

Place	Date	Hour	Summary of Events and Information	Remarks and references to Appendices
DOMART en PONTHIEU	28.X.15		No 2 Sec. Brigade Field Day. No 3 Sec. Section marched from BEAUVAL to RIBEAUCOURT arriving 2.30 p.m. Office opened at 4 p.m. and line to H.Q. taken over. Communication to Bde. by cyclists. No 4 Sec. Attached 12th Bde. for Training. H.Q. & No 1 Sec. Telephone line to Div Train at MONTRELET faulty. Adjusted at 11.30 a.m. No 2 Sec. moved to CANAPLES. Communication maintained during move on Arty. lines - Cable carried on from ST. LEGER to CANAPLES at 8 p.m. Telephone Circuit to No 3 Sec. faulty. No 2 Sec. Section moved to CANAPLES. No 3 Sec. lines laid to 11th R.I.R. at FIENVILLERS, 12th R.I.R. at BERNAVILLE and 13th R.I.R. at BERNAVILLE and communication established at 12 noon. Communication to 9th R.I.R. Bns and 108th Fld. Amb. by D.Rs. Commenced laying line to 108th Fld. Amb. No 4 Sec. Attached 12th Bde. for Training.	
DOMART en PONTHIEU	29.X.15		H.Q. & No 1 Sec. Telephone Circuit to No 3 Sec. still faulty. Repaired by 12 noon. Communication otherwise good. No 2 Sec. Trench Telephone communication to H.Q. through French exchange at CANAPLES. No 3 Sec. Communication by cable to 9th R.I.R. Bns and 108 Fld. Amb. opened at 8.30 a.m. No 4 Sec. Attached 12th Bde. for Training.	

Army Form C. 2118.

36th Signal Coy. R.E.

WAR DIARY
or
INTELLIGENCE SUMMARY.
(Erase heading not required.)

Instructions regarding War Diaries and Intelligence Summaries are contained in F.S. Regs., Part II. and the Staff Manual respectively. Title pages will be prepared in manuscript.

Place	Date	Hour	Summary of Events and Information	Remarks and references to Appendices
DOMART en PONTHIEU	30.X.15		H.Q. & No 1 Sec. Communications satisfactory. Connected French mission to 36th Div. H.A. by telephone	
			No 2 Sec. Lines satisfactory owing to induction from Artillery lines	
			No 3 Sec. Communications good.	
			No 4 Sec. 10th Bde. relieved 12th Bde. Section attached 10th Bde. for training	
DOMART en PONTHIEU	31.X.15		H.Q. & No 1 Sec. Nothing to report. Lines satisfactory	
			No 2 Sec. Lines working satisfactorily	
			No 3 Sec. Communications good	
			No 4 Sec. attached 10th Bde. for training	

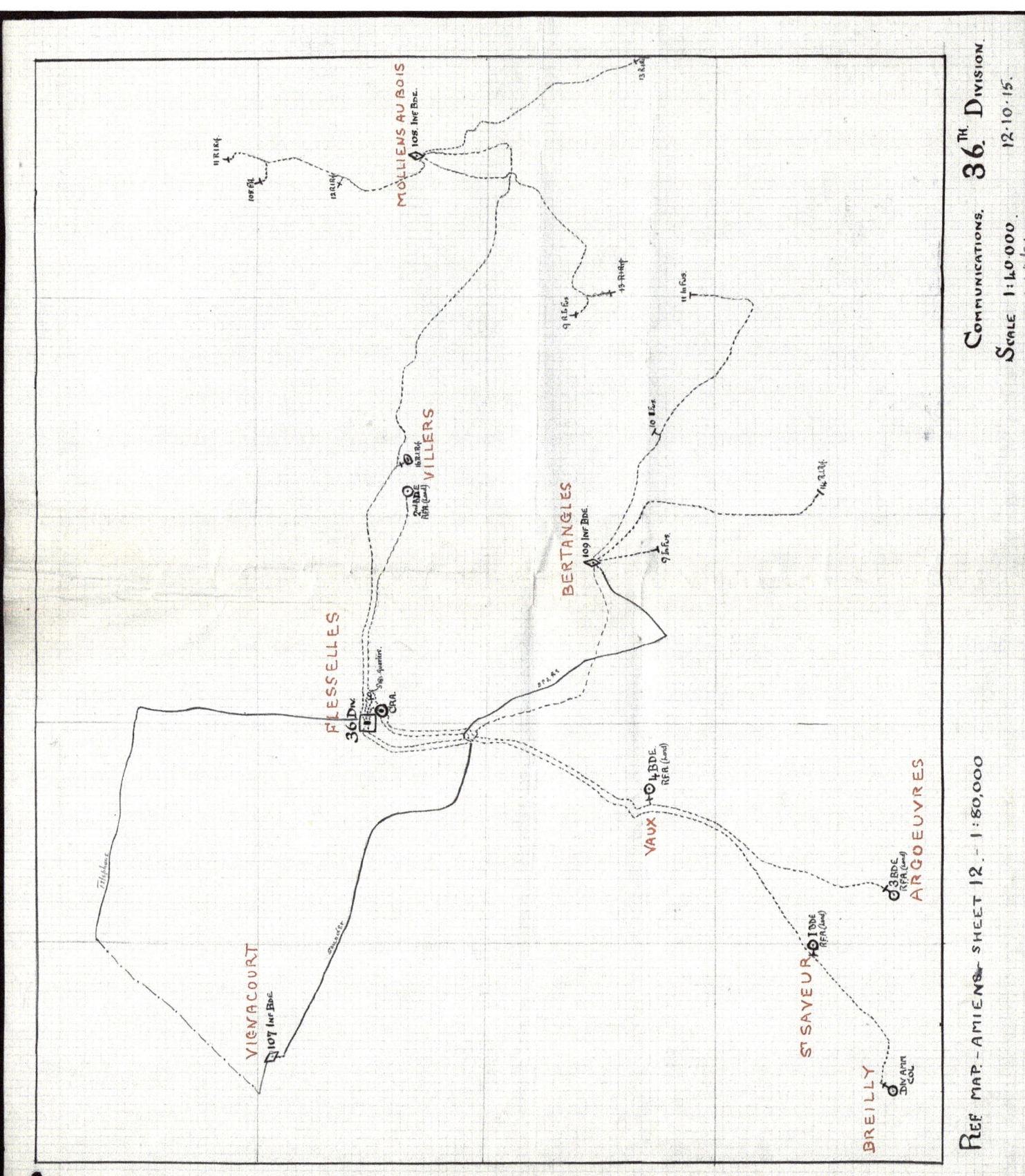

36th div: Sig: Coy: R.E.
Vol: 2

121/7693

Nov. 15

CONFIDENTIAL

WAR DIARY

36th Divisional Signal Company, Royal Engineers.

from

1st November, 1915 To 31st November, 1915

VOLUME TWO

Army Form C. 2118.

WAR DIARY
or
INTELLIGENCE SUMMARY.
(Erase heading not required.)

36th Div. Sig. Co. R.E.

Instructions regarding War Diaries and Intelligence Summaries are contained in F. S. Regs., Part II. and the Staff Manual respectively. Title pages will be prepared in manuscript.

Place	Date	Hour	Summary of Events and Information	Remarks and references to Appendices
DOMART en PONTHIEU	1.11.15		H.Q. & No 1 Sec. Communications satisfactory. Telephone circuit from H.Q. 36 Div to Div. Arty. faulty at 5.30 p.m. to 6.30 p.m. 15 mins service was resumed.	
			No 2 Sec. nothing to report	
			No 3 Sec. all lines satisfactory	
			No 4 Sec. attached 12th Inf. Bde.	
DOMART en PONTHIEU	2.11.15		H.Q. & No 1 Sec. lines working satisfactorily	
			No 2 Sec. nothing to report	
			No 3 Sec. 5.25 a.m. to 7 a.m. Line to 11th R.I.R. dis broken in 2 places. 7.10 a.m. to 7.35 a.m. wire to 108 Fd. Amb. dis. All other lines satisfactory	
			No 4 Sec. attached 12th Inf. Bde. Sections recalled from report centre	
DOMART en PONTHIEU	3.11.15		H.Q. & No 1 Sec. 9 a.m. to 9.20 a.m. wire to VII Corps dis. Erection of aerial air line to BEAUVAL continued	
			No 2 Sec. moved out to take place of 12th Inf. Bde. moving into 36th Div. area	
			No 3 Sec. lines satisfactory	
			No 4 Sec. marched back from 12th Inf. Bde. to 36th Div. Area (BEAUVAL)	
DOMART en PONTHIEU	4.11.15		H.Q. & No 1 Sec. Satisfactory - nothing to report	
			No 2 Sec. moved into 4th Div. Training area	

WAR DIARY or INTELLIGENCE SUMMARY

Army Form C. 2118.

Place	Date	Hour	Summary of Events and Information	Remarks and references to Appendices
DOMART en PONTHIEU	6.11.15		No 3 Sec. Lines satisfactory. 5.35 p.m. piece of R.F.R. between places autoped. at spare line to 108 2nd Ind dis from 7.30 to 9.30 am otherwise satisfactory.	
			No 4 Sec. line laid to 9th R. Munn. Brie from CANDAS to LONGUEVILETTE	
			H.Q. & No 1 Sec. line to 3rd Army dis from 12.30 to 12.50 p.m. Communication to LUCKNOW Casualty Clearing Station at ST. OUEN at 5 pm. Telephone circuit D3 cable laid by 3rd Army. French minimum connected to Switchboard in this office.	
			No 2 Sec. Communications satisfactory	
			No 3 Sec. Communication with heavy arms at FIENVILLERS opened at 1.50 p.m. Other lines good	
			No 4 Sec. Direct line from Sig. Office (BEAUVAL) laid to 9th R. Muns. Bri. at LONGUEVILLETTE	
DOMART en PONTHIEU	5.11.15		H.Q. & No 1 Sec. Communications good	
			No 2 Sec. moved to 4th Div. Training area – 12th Bde. moved into 36th Bde area & took place of 107 Bde.	
			No 3 Sec. Communications working well.	
			No 4 Sec. line to 11th R. Munn. Bris. put up on Poles	
DOMART en PONTHIEU	7.11.15		H.Q. & No 1 Sec. Satisfactory	
			No 2 Sec. attached 4th Div.	
			No 3 Sec. lines all good.	

Army Form C. 2118.

36th Signal Coy. R.E.

WAR DIARY
or
INTELLIGENCE SUMMARY.
(Erase heading not required.)

Instructions regarding War Diaries and Intelligence Summaries are contained in F.S. Regs., Part II. and the Staff Manual respectively. Title pages will be prepared in manuscript.

Place	Date	Hour	Summary of Events and Information	Remarks and references to Appendices
DOMART en PONTHIEU	8.11.15		No 4 Sec. lines satisfactory	
			H.Q. & No 1 Sec. Communications working satisfactorily	
			No 2 Sec. attached 4th Div.	
			No 3 Sec. lines all satisfactory	
			No 4 Sec. Visual communication established with 11th R. Innis. Inns. at GANDAS	
DOMART en PONTHIEU	9.11.15		H.Q. & No 1 Sec. Induction on telephone line to B6 10" Train at MONTRELET, otherwise satisfactory	
			No 2 Sec. attached 4th Div.	
			No 3 Sec. Satisfactory	
			No 4 Sec. Signal Office received Communications 900	
DOMART en PONTHIEU	10.11.15		H.Q. & No 1 Sec. Communications good	
			No 2 Sec. attached 4th Div.	
			No 3 Sec. Satisfactory	
			No 4 Sec. nothing to report	
			12th Bde. Sec. nothing to report.	
DOMART en PONTHIEU	11.11.15		H.Q. & No 1 Sec. nothing to report	
			No 2 Sec. attached 4th Div.	

Army Form C. 2118.

36th Signal Coy R.E.

WAR DIARY
or
INTELLIGENCE SUMMARY.
(Erase heading not required.)

Instructions regarding War Diaries and Intelligence Summaries are contained in F. S. Regs., Part II. and the Staff Manual respectively. Title pages will be prepared in manuscript.

Place	Date	Hour	Summary of Events and Information	Remarks and references to Appendices
DOMART en	12.11.15		No 3 Sec - lines working satisfactory	
			No 4 Sec. Communication by Telephone established to 10th R.Innis Bns & 2nd Essex Regt.	
PONTHIEU			12th Bde. Sec. No 4. Sig. Officer (Lt. BEAUMONT) proceeded on leave Lieut. Hunt. Satisfactory	
			H.Q. & No 1 Sec. lines working well. Coy M.S. Stratton evacuated to Div. Rest Camp	
			No 2 Sec. All? 4th Divs	
			No 3 Sec. Satisfactory	
			No 4 Sec. Telephone communication established to 109 Fd. Amb. Commenced laying line to GEZAINCOURT near H.Q. of 9th R.Innis Fus.	
			12th Bde. No 4 Sec. nothing to report	
DOMART en	13.11.15		H.Q. & No 1 Sec. nothing to report	
PONTHIEU			No 2 Sec. All? 4th Divr	
			12 Bde. No 4 Sec. nothing to report	
			No 3 Sec. Line to 2nd Lanc. Fus. dis. from 10.30 a.m. to 12.15 p.m. Others satisfactory	
			No 4 Sec. Line to 9th R.Innis Bns. at GEZAINCOURT finished	
DOMART en	14.11.15		H.Q. & No 1 Sec. All lines satisfactory	
PONTHIEU			No 2 Sec. All? 4th Divr	

36th Signal Co. R.E.

Army Form C. 2118.

WAR DIARY
or
INTELLIGENCE SUMMARY.
(Erase heading not required.)

Instructions regarding War Diaries and Intelligence Summaries are contained in F. S. Regs., Part II. and the Staff Manual respectively. Title pages will be prepared in manuscript.

Place	Date	Hour	Summary of Events and Information	Remarks and references to Appendices
DOMART en PONTHIEU	15/11/15		No 3 Sec. No 4 Sec. 12th Bde. No 4 Sec. } Nothing to report. H.Q. & No 1 Sec. Nothing to report. No 2 Sec. All? 4th Div. No 3 Sec. H.Q. & 3 Bns. moved into 4th & 8th Div. Bde. Areas. Sig. Office 9th R.I.R. Bns. closed at 10 a.m. 13th R.I.R. at 2.30 p.m. and 12th R.I.R. at 2.45 p.m. H.Q. Sig. Office remained at RIBEAUCOURT. Motor cyclist and 2 Cyclist O.Rs. accompanied Bde. H.Q. No 4 Sec. Line to 9th R. Innis. Bns. at LONGUEVILLETTE rolled up. 12th Bde. No 4 Sec. Lines satisfactory	
DOMART en PONTHIEU	16/11/15		H.Q. & No 1 Sec. Lines satisfactory. Alteration in hours of Posts 15 Roles — hrs to Corps Army machine ⊙ No 2 Sec. All? 4th Div. No 3 Sec. Lines satisfactory No 4 Sec. Line between CANDAS & LONGUEVILLETTE 12th Bde. No 4 Sec. Nothing to report.	
DOMART en PONTHIEU	17/11/15		H.Q. & all Sections (including 12th Bde. No 4 Sec.). All lines working satisfactorily.	

1577 Wt.W10791/1773 500,000 1/15 D.D.&L. A.D.S.S./Forms/C. 2118.

Army Form C. 2118.

WAR DIARY
or
INTELLIGENCE SUMMARY.
(Erase heading not required.)

36th Signal Co. R.E.

Instructions regarding War Diaries and Intelligence Summaries are contained in F.S. Regs, Part II. and the Staff Manual respectively. Title pages will be prepared in manuscript.

Place	Date	Hour	Summary of Events and Information	Remarks and references to Appendices
DOMART en PONTHIEU	18.11.15		H.Q. & No 1 Sec. 36th Div. posts to 13th Corps at DOULLENS Telephone & Telegraph circuit changed to DOULLENS. Communication to 7th Corps direct, closed. No 2 Sec. att'd 4th Div. No 3 Sec. Communication good. No 4 Sec. (Portion of line to 11th R. Innis. Bde. relaid to avoid induction. 12th Bde. & No 4 Sec. nothing to report.	
DOMART en PONTHIEU	19.11.15		H.Q. & No 1 Sec. Instruments to 7th Corps & 3rd Army removed by 7th Corps & replaced by 13th Corps. No 1, 3, 4 & 12th Bde. No 4 Sec. Satisfactory. No 2 Sec. att'd 4th Div.	
DOMART en PONTHIEU	20.11.15		H.Q. No 1 Sec, No 4 Sec & 12th Bde. No 4 Sec. Communications good. No 2 Sec. att'd 4th Div. No 2 Sec. line to Lanc. Bn. Hrs. 1.50 p.m. to 3.40 p.m. Line broken.	
DOMART en PONTHIEU	21.11.15		H.Q. and all Sections - Communication satisfactory. 3 men of No 1 Sec. admitted to Hospital. No 2 Sec. att'd 4th Div.	
DOMART en PONTHIEU	22.11.15		H.Q. and all Sections - nothing to report. Communication good. No 2 Sec. att'd 4th Div.	

36th Signal Co. 4 R.E.

Army Form C. 2118.

WAR DIARY
or
INTELLIGENCE SUMMARY.
(Erase heading not required.)

Instructions regarding War Diaries and Intelligence Summaries are contained in F.S. Regs., Part II. and the Staff Manual respectively. Title pages will be prepared in manuscript.

Place	Date	Hour	Summary of Events and Information	Remarks and references to Appendices
DOMART en PONTHIEU	23.11.15		H.Q. and all Sections. Communications satisfactory. No 2 Sec. attached 4th Div.	
DOMART en PONTHIEU	24.11.15		H.Q. & No 1 Sec. move line to III Army out of order from 10 am to 4 pm. Built from III Army Signal Office. No 2 Sec. attached 4th Div.	
DOMART en PONTHIEU	25.11.15		H.Q. & all sections - Lines working satisfactorily. Corrie Air line commenced in new area. No 2 Sec. att? 4th Div. 12th Bde. Sec. no report. No 3 Sec. March back to Bde. area commenced after period of training in Trenches.	
DOMART en PONTHIEU	26.11.15		H.Q. & No 1 Sec. Conveyment on move of Div. to new area. Line to Huckarow Clearing Stn. ruled up. Telephone communication to 108th Bde. ruled up. III Army at 3pm. Corrie Air line to new area resumed. No 2 Sec att? 4th Div. 12th Bde. Sec. no report. No 3 Sec. 108th Bde. returned from Trenches. Communications opened with 12th & 13th R.Ir. Rifles and 9th R. In. Div. opened up. No 4 Sec. a second Offmove of Div. all lines ruled up. Telephone Comm? thro' BEAUVAL exchange commuted.	

1577 Wt. W10791/1773 500,000 1/15 D.D.&L. A.D.S.S./Forms/C. 2118.

36th Signal Co. R.E.

WAR DIARY or INTELLIGENCE SUMMARY.
Army Form C. 2118.

(Erase heading not required.)

Instructions regarding War Diaries and Intelligence Summaries are contained in F. S. Regs., Part II. and the Staff Manual respectively. Title pages will be prepared in manuscript.

Place	Date	Hour	Summary of Events and Information	Remarks and references to Appendices
DOMART en PONTHIEU	27.11.15		at 3 p.m. Direct line to Div. dismantled at 12 mid. H.Q. & No 1 Sec. Party went to PONT REMY to prepare offices and connect lines previously prepared. Comn. to PONT REMY at 4 p.m. & on to 108th Rgt. at ST. RIQUIER, 109th Bde. at AILLY LE HAUT CLOCHER and 32nd Div. at same place. No 2 Sec. attached 4th Div. 12th Bde. Sec. Bde. & Bn. Offices closed. Marched to HOUDENCOURT. No 2 Sec. Bde. Office closed at 8.10 a.m. Lines reeled up. Office opened at ST. RIQUIER at 4 p.m. Comn. commenced with 36th Div. & 13th R.I. Rgt. No 4 Sec. Bde. arr. GORENFLOS at 1.30 p.m. Communication with Div. commenced & opened up with 11th R. Inniskilling Fus. at DOMQUEUR and 10th R. Inniskilling Fus. at GORENFLOS, 9th R. Innis. Fus. at BRUCAMPS.	
DOMART en PONTHIEU	28.11.15		H.Q. & No 1 Sec. line to III Army Div. 8.45 a.m. to 9 a.m. line to 13th Corps removed from hut at 11 a.m. & new (other) from hair of Comic Run. lines working to Army Corps through III Army. 12th Bde. Sec. No report. No 3 Sec. Communication established with 2nd Hants. Bn. at ST. MAUGUVILLE at 9 a.m., 9th R.I. Bn. at BELLANCOURT at 2 p.m., 12th R.I. Rgt. at VAUCHELLES-LES-QUESNEY at 4.15 p.m. No 4 Sec. Communication with 10th R. Innis. Bn. at GORENFLOS.	

36th Signal Co. R.E.

Army Form C. 2118.

WAR DIARY
or
INTELLIGENCE SUMMARY.
(Erase heading not required.)

Instructions regarding War Diaries and Intelligence Summaries are contained in F. S. Regs., Part II. and the Staff Manual respectively. Title pages will be prepared in manuscript.

Place	Date	Hour	Summary of Events and Information	Remarks and references to Appendices
PONT REMY	29.11.15		H.Q. & No 1 Sec. Office closed at DOMART & PONTHIEU at 11 am & opened at PONT REMY at same time working to 13th Corps through ABBEVILLE. Commenced air line to DOMART disconnected. Communication opened with 12th Bde, 108th Bde, 109th Bde, 36th Div. R.A., Veterinary Ambulance, 13th Corps and 36th Div. Train. 12th Bde. No report. No 3 Sec. line to 2nd Lanc. Gun. dis. 8.50 am to 9.15 am. No 4 Sec. line to 108th Bde. Amb. commenced at LA HAIE. F.E.	
PONT REMY	30.11.15		H.Q. & No 1 Sec. Communications satisfactory. Direct communication to 13th Corps at DOMART commenced. No 2 Sec. still at? 4th Div. No 3 Sec. line to 12th R.H. Rig and 9th R.L. Gun. dis. from 11.30 am to 2.20 pm. No 4 Sec. Communication with 108th Bde Amb. established.	

E. A. Prentice Major
O.C. 36th Signal Co. R.E.

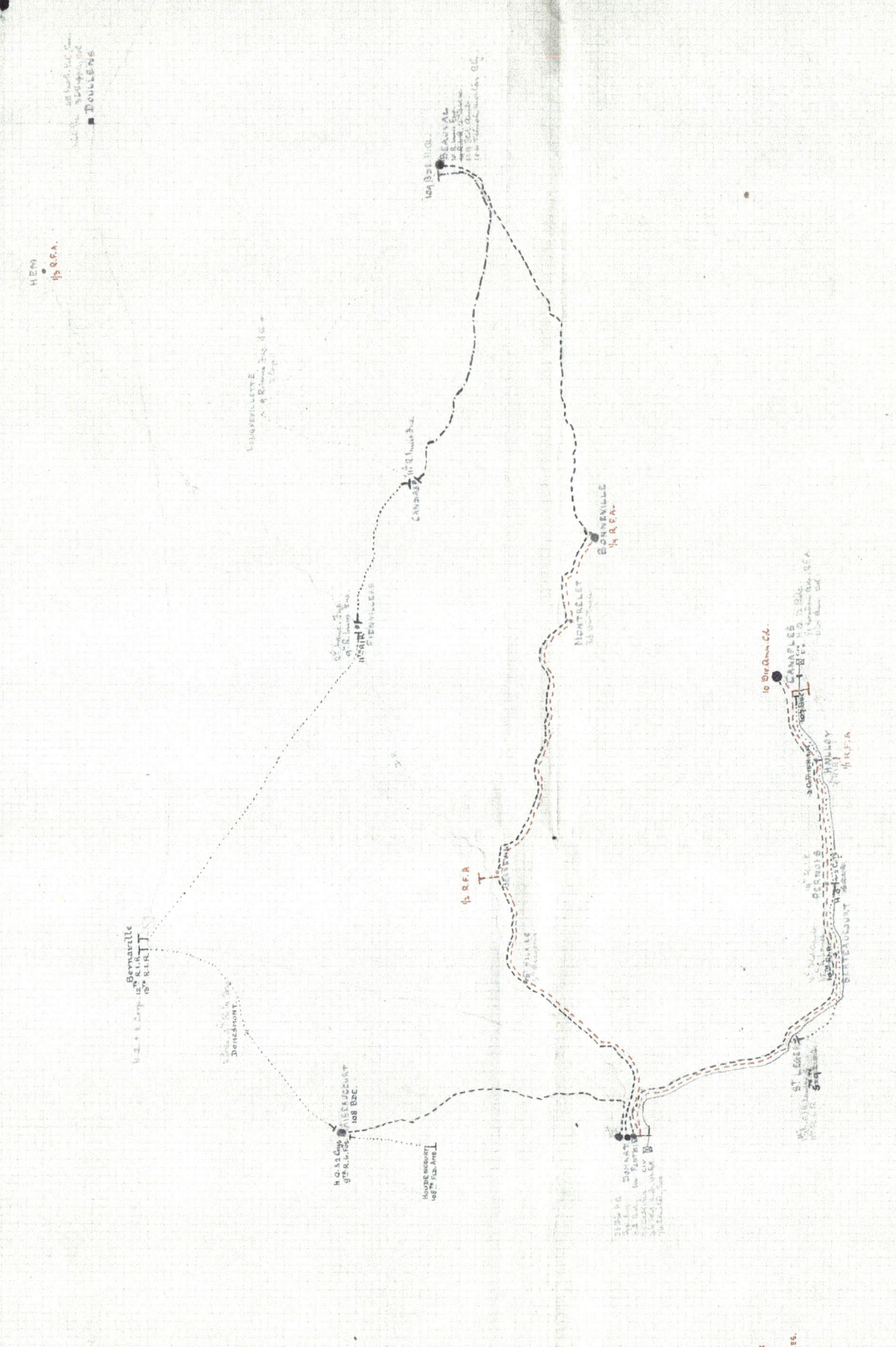

Communications 36th Signal Company

36ñ Sri: Sri: Gupte.
Vol: 3

9904/
19/

CONFIDENTIAL

WAR DIARY

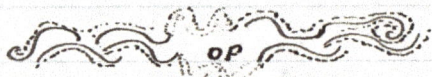

36th DIVISIONAL SIGNAL COMPANY R.E.

━━ FROM ━━

1st DECEMBER, 1915.

━━ TO ━━

31st DECEMBER, 1915.

VOLUME ———— THREE.

36th Signal Company R.E.   Army Form C. 2118.

WAR DIARY
or
INTELLIGENCE SUMMARY.
(Erase heading not required.)

Instructions regarding War Diaries and Intelligence Summaries are contained in F. S. Regs., Part II. and the Staff Manual respectively. Title pages will be prepared in manuscript.

Place	Date	Hour	Summary of Events and Information	Remarks and references to Appendices
PONT REMY	1.12.15		No. 1 & No. 1 Sec here to 13th Corps causing trouble owing to interruption of send from Sprader apparatus on the line	
			No 2 Sec all[?] 4th 10 ip	
		✕	12th Bde Sec no report	
			No 3 Sec here to 12th & 15th Div. Rep of R/T. Sec dis from 7.10 am & 7.30 am and from 2.30 pm to 4 pm	
			No 4 Sec Satisfactory	
PONT REMY	2.12.15		H.Q. & no 1 Sec Telephone circuit 15 & 13th Corps giving trouble. One attachment "B" No 1 Sec sent to BEAUVAL and one Sec to MONTRELET & rest up cable	
			Nos 2, 3 & 4 Secs Communications on all lines satisfactory	
PONT REMY	3.12.15		H.Q. & No 1 Sec All lines satisfactory. Detachments from BEAUVAL & MONTRELET returned	
			Nos 2, 3 & 4 Sec nothing to report	
PONT REMY	4.12.15		H.Q. & No 1 Sec here to 13th Corps dis from 10.6 11 am & from 5.15 to 6 pm - Two air line sections from PONT REMY to ST RIQUIER	
			13th Corps laid a Cross air line from PONT REMY to ST RIQUIER	
			Nos 2, 3 & 4 Secs lines satisfactory	
PONT REMY[?] to[?] [?]	[?]		H.Q. & No 1 Sec here to 13th Corps dis from 10.25[?] to 11.25 am & from 12.45 to 5 pm. 13th Corps Commander ✕ No Cable will be made which No Sec is attached to 4th Div. In future No 2 Sec will refer to the Sec of 12th Bde which is attached to the same	

36th Signal Co. R.E.

Army Form C. 2118

WAR DIARY
or
INTELLIGENCE SUMMARY.
(Erase heading not required.)

Place	Date	Hour	Summary of Events and Information	Remarks and references to Appendices
PONT REMY	5.12.15		Working on his line. Nos 2, 3 & 4 Sects. lines satisfactory. H.Q. & No 1 Sec. line to 13th Corps dis. from 11.5-11.25 a.m. again from 12 to 6.15 p.m. line to 108 Bde dis from 10.50 a.m to 12.10 p.m. owing to change of lines. Nos 2 & 4 Secs. nothing to report. No 3 Sec. communication established with No 3 Coy. A.S.C. at 4.40 p.m.	
PONT REMY	6.12.15		H.Q. & No 1 Sec. line to 109 Bde dis. from 5.10 p.m to 6.15 p.m. Communication established with 36th (Ulster) Div. Supply Col. at L'ETOILE through PONT REMY Civil Exchange – 36th Div. Artillery moved from FRANCIERES to COCQUEREL – line laid into 36th Div. Arty. ætt line – communication opened at 12.20 p.m. Nos 2, 3 & 4 Secs. Satisfactory.	
PONT REMY	7.12.15		H.Q. & No 1 See. line to 108 Bde. dis from 9.15 a.m. to 12.20 p.m. Nos 2 & 4 Secs. nothing to report. No 3 Sec. line to 36th Div. H.Q. dis from 9.15 a.m. to 12.20 p.m.	
PONT REMY	8.12.15		H.Q. & No 1 Sec. Communications satisfactory – Counter-air line being put up to replace Cable – One Riding Horse of No 1 Sec. died.	

36th Signal Co. 4 R.E.

Army Form C. 2118

WAR DIARY
or
INTELLIGENCE SUMMARY.
(Erase heading not required.)

Instructions regarding War Diaries and Intelligence Summaries are contained in F.S. Regs., Part II. and the Staff Manual respectively. Title pages will be prepared in manuscript.

Place	Date	Hour	Summary of Events and Information	Remarks and references to Appendices
PONT REMY	9.12.15		No 2 & 3 Secs. Communications satisfactory	
			No 4 Sec. lines 15-10th R.Innis. Bn. and 2nd Essex R. tested in and replaced by enamelled wire. One Officer's charger in this Section died	
PONT REMY	10.12.15		H.Q. & No 1. Sec. Erection of Comic Air line to replace Cable continued. All lines satisfactory	
			No 2 & 3 Sec. Lines satisfactory	
			No 4 Sec. Cable to 9th R.Innis. Bn. repaired by Comic Air line	
			H.Q. & No 1. Sec. Satisfactory	
			No 2 Sec. Comic Air line put up from (K.O.) Lane R. to S. Lane. Bn. — 2nd Lane. Bn. and Essex R. joined Their Bde in place of 11th and 14th R.I. Rifles and Signal Wires handed over.	
			No 3 Sec. Comic Air line from ST RIQUIER to BELLANCOURT commenced. 2nd lines Bn. rejoined 12th Bde. and 11th R.I. Rif. returned	
			No 4 Sec. Comic Air line to 9th R.Innis. Bn. completed. 3rd Essex R. rejoined 12th Bde and 14th R.I. Rif. returned	
PONT REMY	11.12.15		H.Q. & No 1 Sec. All communications satisfactory	
			No 2 Sec. Nothing to report	
			No 3 Sec. Comic Air line to 9th & 12th R.I. Rif. continued. line 11th R.I. Rif. dis from 11.45 am to 12.10 pm	

1577 Wt.W10791/1773 500,000 1/15 D.D.&L. A.D.S.S./Forms/C. 2118.

36th Signal Coy R.E.

Army Form C. 2118

WAR DIARY
or
INTELLIGENCE SUMMARY.
(Erase heading not required.)

Instructions regarding War Diaries and Intelligence Summaries are contained in F. S. Regs., Part II. and the Staff Manual respectively. Title pages will be prepared in manuscript.

Place	Date	Hour	Summary of Events and Information	Remarks and references to Appendices
PONT REMY	12.12.15		H.Q. + No 1 Sec. 36th Div. Arty (T.F.) left Bivouac area. Officer closed down. Work in Comms. Air line completed.	
			No 2 & 3 Sec. Communications satisfactory	
			No 4 Sec. Comms. Air line to 15th R. Horse Arty. completed	
PONT REMY	13.12.15		H.Q. + No 1 Sec. lines working satisfactorily	
			No 2 Sec. Nothing to report	
			No 3 Sec. Communications good	
			No 4 Sec. Comms. Air line to 108 Bde Amn. completed and cable reels up. All cable lines in 109 Bde now replaced by Comms. air line or enamelled wire.	
PONT REMY	14.12.15		H.Q. + No 1 Sec. line to 109 Bde dis. from 2.45 to 3.55 p.m. otherwise satisfactory	
			No 2 Sec. Comms. Air line to Lane Ins. finished - line to K.O. Lane Regt. dis. from 11.55 a.m. to 1.30 p.m.	
			out by plough.	
			No 3 Sec. + No 4 Sec. communications satisfactory	
PONT REMY	15.12.15		H.Q. + No 1 Sec. Communications Satisfactory. 95th + 104th Trench Mortar Battery left Div. area joined	
			Adv. Base Signal Depot on discharge from hospital and struck off strength	
			No 2, 3 + 4 Sec. Nothing to report.	

36th Signal Co 4 R.E.

WAR DIARY
or
INTELLIGENCE SUMMARY.

Army Form C. 2118

Instructions regarding War Diaries and Intelligence Summaries are contained in F. S. Regs., Part II. and the Staff Manual respectively. Title pages will be prepared in manuscript.

(Erase heading not required.)

Place	Date	Hour	Summary of Events and Information	Remarks and references to Appendices
PONT REMY	16.12.15		H.Q. & No 1 Section - nothing to report	
			Nos 2, 3 & 4 Sections - communications satisfactory	
PONT REMY	17.12.15		H.Q. & No 1 Section - line to 108 Bde phs. from 2.15pm to 4.15pm. Cut by a Barge - Otherwise Satisfactory	
			No 2 Sec. Two miles of Cable replaced by Comic Air line	
			No 3 Sec. line to 15 Div. dis from 2.15pm to 4.15pm	
			No 4 Sec. Office to 108 Bde. Closed owing to small amount of Traffic. Telephone communication	
			to No 4 Coy. A.S.C. and 108 Bde. Amb. commenced.	
PONT REMY	18.12.15		H.Q. & No 1 Sec. Riding Horse of No 1 Sec. died. Replaced by one from 48 North Vet Sec.	
			No 2 Sec. nothing to report	
			No 3 Sec. line to 5th R.h. Fro. and 12 R.h. Rif. dis. from 9.15pm to 10.45pm.	
			No 4 Sec. nothing to report	
PONT REMY	19.12.15		H.Q. & No 1 Sec. line to 108 Bde dis. from 2 p.m. to 6.25 p.m.	
			Nos 2 & 4 Secs. nothing to report	
			No 3 Sec. 15 Div. line dis from 2 p.m to 6.25 p.m.	
PONT REMY	20.12.15		H.Q. and all Sections - nothing to report. All communications satisfactory.	
PONT REMY	21.12.15		H.Q. and all Sections - do - do -	

1577 Wt.W10791/1773 500,000 1/15 D. D. & L. A.D.S.S./Forms/C. 2118.

36th Signal Co. 4 R.E.

Army Form C. 2118

WAR DIARY
or
INTELLIGENCE SUMMARY.
(Erase heading not required.)

Instructions regarding War Diaries and Intelligence Summaries are contained in F. S. Regs., Part II. and the Staff Manual respectively. Title pages will be prepared in manuscript.

Place	Date	Hour	Summary of Events and Information	Remarks and references to Appendices
PONT REMY	22.12.15		H.Q. and all Sections. All communications satisfactory.	
PONT REMY	23.12.15		H.Q. and all Sections. All communications satisfactory.	
PONT REMY	24.12.15		H.Q. and all Sections. Nothing to report. All lines good.	
PONT REMY	25.12.15		H.Q. and all Sections. Satisfactory. 16-20 Wolseley Car arrived in place of "Light" Singer Car. No 14/2/11074. Pte. G.H.Tyler (Chauffeur) taken on strength.	
PONT REMY	26.12.15		H.Q. and all Sections - lines satisfactory	
PONT REMY	27.12.15		H.Q. - line to 109 Bde. breaking at 10.35 a.m. - Sounder unworkable owing to very weak Signals. Messages transmitted by Telephone. Fault repaired at 12.15 p.m. by substituting lead of Cable at 109 Bde. end by length of bare wire - line to 12th Bde. faulty but communication not interrupted. Instrument repairer sent out. No 1 Sec. 1h.C.O. and 2 men sent to 7th Corps for course of instruction as knees men. Nos 2, 3 + 4 Secs. Satisfactory.	
PONT REMY	28.12.15		H.Q. line to 12th Bde. made right and communication satisfactory. Nos 1, 2 + 3 Sectn. lines satisfactory. No 4 Sec. Gun crew of 53rd (Welsh) Div. Arty. for temporary attachment to this Sec. communication established with their H.Q. at LONGVILLERS by running D/Cable line from H.Q. of R. Innis. Fus. at	

1577 Wt.W10791/1773 500,000 1/15 D. D. & L. A.D.S.S./Forms/C. 2118.

36th Signal Co. R.E.

Army Form C. 2118

WAR DIARY
or
INTELLIGENCE SUMMARY.
(Erase heading not required.)

Place	Date	Hour	Summary of Events and Information	Remarks and references to Appendices
PONT REMY	29.12.15		DOMQUEUR wire linking him up with Div. Communication opened 5.30 pm. H.Q. line to 109 Bde. dis. from 8.45 am. to 9.15 a.m. N.C. Corp Scott evacuated to Motor Ambulance Convoy Clearing Station as a result of injuries sustained whilst mending on D.R. No 1, 2 & 3 Secs. nothing to report. No 4 Sec. Comic air line to 11th R.I. Musi. Bn. completed. Communication to 14th R.I. Reg. established by testing on to his line.	
PONT REMY	30.12.15		H.Q. to No 1, 3 & 4 Secs. Satisfactory. No 2 Sec. Comic Air line to K.O.R. Lanc. Regt completed.	
PONT REMY	31.12.15		H.Q. Following reinforcements arrived from Signal Depot (ABBEVILLE) No 57826 2/c N.C. Mahoney No 57975 Pte R. Bell. Whom on strength and posted to No 3 Sec. Nos 1, 3 & 4 Secs. Communications satisfactory. No 2 Sec. Telephone Commn to Bn. suspended between 9 a.m. & 3 p.m. owing to Brigade Scheme. All messages sent by visual.	

E. a. Parker Major
Commanding 36th Signal Company R.E.

Communications 36th Signal Company R.E.

Legend:
- Black .... Divisional lines
- Red .... Artillery lines
- Green .... Brigade lines
- E.W. .... Transmitted wire
- O .... Visual
- T .... D III
- ↙ .... Sounder

Locations and Units:

- **Longvillers** — H.Q. 55 Bde R.A, 4 Welsh F.A. Bde
- **Fransu** — 15 D.A.C.
- **Domqueur** — HQ Welsh Bde R.A., 9 R. Innis. Fus, 150 Fld. Co.
- **Franqueville** — T Welsh F.A. Bde
- **Gorenflos** — HQ 109 Bde, 10 R. Innis. Fus, 109 T.M. Bty
- **To Domart en Ponthieu**
- **La Haie Ts** — 108 Fld. Amb.
- **Surcamps** — 251 G. A.S.C.
- **Coulomvillers** — 1/5 S. Lanc. R.
- **Ergnies** — 11 R.I.Fus.
- **Brucamps** — 11 R. Innis. Fus
- **Vauchelle-les Domart**
- **Moufflers** — 172 Bde R.A.
- **Bussus-Bussue** — 1st K.O.R. Lancs.
- **St Riquier** — H.Q. 108 Bde, 13 R.Ir. Rif, 4 S T.M. Bty
- **St Maquille** — 255 G.A.S.C., 11 R.Ir. Rif.
- **Bugny L'Abbé** — 2 R. Lanc. Fus.
- **Ailly le haut Clocher** — H.Q. 12 Bde, 2 Essex R., 8 T.M. Bty
- **Vauchelles les Quesnoy** — 12 R.Ir. Rif.
- **Bellancourt** — 9 R.Ir. Fus, 118 Mob. Vet. Sec.
- **To Abbeville**
- **Pont Remy** — H.Q. 36 Div., C.R.E., 109 Fld. Amb., 76 San. Sec., 36 Fld. Amb. W'shps., 36 Cyclists.
- **Cocquerel**
- **Long** — H.Q. 153 Bde R.A., 251 G. A.S.C., 153 Bde R.A.
- **Bouchon** — 173 Bde R.A.
- **L'Etoile** — 36 Div Supply Col.
- **Bethencourt** — Cheshire F.A. Bde

Scale 1 : 80,000

Mile ½ 0 1 2 3 4 5 Miles

36th Div: Spiale
Vol: 4

CONFIDENTIAL

WAR DIARY

36th Divisional Signal Company, Royal Engineers.

From ~~~~~~ 1st January, 1916
To ~~~~~~ 31st January, 1916.

Volume........Four.

36th Signal Co^y R.E.

Army Form C. 2118.

WAR DIARY
or
INTELLIGENCE SUMMARY.
(Erase heading not required.)

Instructions regarding War Diaries and Intelligence Summaries are contained in F. S. Regs., Part II. and the Staff Manual respectively. Title pages will be prepared in manuscript.

Place	Date	Hour	Summary of Events and Information	Remarks and references to Appendices
PONT REMY	1.1.16		H.Q. No 57652 N.O. Corp C.F. Norris reinforced from Depot taken on strength of Coy. Owing to a storm last evening Comic Air line to 13th Corps and 108 Bde in contact Comm to Bde (106) interrupted from 5.30 pm to 8 pm. Contact also on R.A. line.	
			No 1 Sec. nothing to report	
			No 2 Sec Cable line to K.O.R. Lanc Regt. picked up, already repaired by Comic	
			No 3 Sec Div. line also from 5.30pm to 8 pm. Line to 11 R.h Regt. down from 5.45 pm to 7 pm	
			No 4 Sec nothing to report	
			H.Q. & all Sections – nothing to report	
PONT REMY	2.1.16			
PONT REMY	3.1.16		H.Q. & No 1 Sec. 16 wounded. N Co. move from PONT REMY to DOMART. Office opened at 12 noon	
DOMART en PONTHIEU			Office in PONT REMY left open	
			No 2, 3 & 4 Sec. Communications retaphoton	
PONT REMY	4.1.16		H.Q. Tel. line Telephone Exchange failed up to replace one belonging to 13th Corps. Local Telephone circuits connected to Exchange. Telephone connected in line to 24th Div. and R.T.O. at LONG PRE preceding up purpose	Diagram attached I annexed
DOMART en PONTHIEU			No See Cable line to RISENCOURT laid for connecting up 108 Bde on arrival. Iron Cross Rd connected to Telephone through Exchange exchange	
			No 2, 3 & 4 Sections. Work retaphoton	

36th Div Signal Coy RE

WAR DIARY or INTELLIGENCE SUMMARY

Army Form C. 2118.

Place	Date	Hour	Summary of Events and Information	Remarks and references to Appendices
PONT REMY DOMART en PONTHIEU	5.1.16		No 4 + No 1 Sec Cable DS laid to RIBEAUCOURT on 4" net made safe Cable DS line laid to FIENVILLERS 10.10g not installed not communication satisfactory. Communication also established with 53rd WELSH Bde H.Q. Vibrator set installed	
			R A at LONGVILLERS. Cable line laid	
			No 2 + 3 Secs nothing to report	
			No 4 Sec. working move to new area, following Officer cloud :- 10" R hans to 8.50 pm - 14" R 1r Ry - 10 pm	
PONT REMY DOMART en PONTHIEU	6.1.16		H Q Sec Vibrator at 10 109th Bde opened by Saunder xii Communications satisfactory	
			Nos 1.2 + 3 Secs lines satisfactory	
			No 4 Sec. Bde Office at GORENFLOS closed at 10 a.m. and opened same hour at FIENVILLERS Communication with all units of Brigade area quite satisfactory	
PONT REMY DOMART en PONTHIEU	7.1.16		H.Q. + No 1 Sec - 108th Bde commenced move to new area. Communication opened on existing line	
			Nos 1, 2, 3 + 4 Secs - nothing to report	
PONT REMY DOMART en PONTHIEU	8.1.16		H Q + No 1 Sec Telephone line changed over to 15 line exchange using 10 line exchange as auxiliary for extra lines. Ten line exchange borrowed from 13 Corps dismantled for return	
			No 2 Sec Line to BUSSUS-BOULONVILLERS not in use, Battalion having moved from here placed line to BUIGNY L'ABBÉ being held by 26th Bde	
			No 3 Sec 107th Bde moved to RIBEAUCOURT today. Office closed at 8.30 a.m. and opened at RIBEAUCOURT at 2 p.m.	

Army Form C. 2118.

36th Div Signal Coy RE

WAR DIARY
or
INTELLIGENCE SUMMARY.
(Erase heading not required.)

Instructions regarding War Diaries and Intelligence Summaries are contained in F. S. Regs., Part II. and the Staff Manual respectively. Title pages will be prepared in manuscript.

Place	Date	Hour	Summary of Events and Information	Remarks and references to Appendices
PONT-REMY sur PONTHIEU	9.1.16		Communication opened with 36th Div, 11th R.Ir.Rif, 53rd Bde R.A, 13th R.Ir.Rif and 9th R.Ir.Fus.	
			No 4 Sec - no report	
			H.Q, no 1, 2 and 3 Sec. nothing to report	
			No 4 Sec. Communication established with 26th Div Supply Col at FIENVILLERS by telephone	
PONT-REMY sur PONTHIEU	10.1.16		H.Q Sec. Line to 13th Corps cancelled - wire to 3rd Army Contact cleared by 3rd Army Communications. Interrupted on 13th Corps Circuit unreliable and all messages sent out - Line from 13th Corps to 30th Div H.Q entry at LE MEILLARD and line to DOMART cut and made a trunk telephone line between 36th Div. Exchange and 13th Corps Exchange.	
			Nos 1, 2, 3 and 4 Secs - nothing to report	
			With the following alterations in the Strength of the Company:-	
			No 57856 Cpl. S. Salt (m.c) proceeded 27.12.15 injuries received in collision	
			No 57955 Pioneer T. Thompson evacuated 26.12.15 injuries received - fell from horse	
			No 57986 Sapper E.W. Cooper evacuated 9.1.16 - sick	
			No 57681 Driver S. Pursley evacuated 16.12.15 sick	
			Reinforcements - No 57975 Pioneer R. Bell 31.12.15 } Both received from Signal Depot R.E. Advanced Base	
			No 57862 Cpl G.F. Warren (In.c) 9.1.16 }	

Army Form C. 2118.

36th Divl Signal Co. R.E

WAR DIARY
or
INTELLIGENCE SUMMARY.

(Erase heading not required.)

Instructions regarding War Diaries and Intelligence Summaries are contained in F. S. Regs., Part II. and the Staff Manual respectively. Title pages will be prepared in manuscript.

Place	Date	Hour	Summary of Events and Information	Remarks and references to Appendices
DOMART en PONTHIEU	11.1.16		No 1, 2 & 4 Secs nothing to report. No 3 Sec Communication opened with 106 Deh Cavdn at VACQUERIE and 12th R.I. R'fg at RIBEAUCOURT.	
DOMART en PONTHIEU	12.1.16		All sections – nothing to report	
DOMART en PONTHIEU	13.1.16		H.Q. Sec Communication to Railhead at LONGPRÉ broken down – eventually repaired but unsatisfactory. No 3 Sec Communication to 3rd Army and 13th Corps in contact – Cleared by 3rd Army Sigs Communication not interrupted but unsatisfactory running to brigades (pedling and lines intermittently in contact. Line to 12th Bde at AILLY & HAUT CLOCHER and to 10th Bde at PONT REMY in contact. Communication to 12th Bde interrupted. Note to 20th Bde in Somerset not unsatisfactory running to Signals pedling – lineman sent out. Nos 1, 2 & 3 Secs nothing to report. No 4 Sec Communications working on Comme Ave line from Bde H.Q. to 16th R.I. R'fg (P) at CANDAS	
DOMART en PONTHIEU	14.1.16		H.Q & No 1 Sec. Morse circuit to 109th Bde discontinued from 9.20 am to 12.30 pm One drum of circuit YCF and CAR (36th Div & 3rd Army) full earth between YCF and BR (duplication) from 10 am to 12.50 pm circuit YCF – ZT (20th Bde) faulty lines in contact with 12th Bde at AILLY and communication restored Bde direct interrupts messages transmitted by 12th Bde at AILLY. Linemen out and fault cleared. No 2 Sec nothing to report	

36th Signal Company R.E.

Army Form C. 2118.

WAR DIARY
or
INTELLIGENCE SUMMARY.
(Erase heading not required.)

Instructions regarding War Diaries and Intelligence Summaries are contained in F. S. Regs., Part II. and the Staff Manual respectively. Title pages will be prepared in manuscript.

Place	Date	Hour	Summary of Events and Information	Remarks and references to Appendices
DOMART en PONTHIEU	15.1.16		No 3 Sec Commander toured with 121st Sig Coy. R.E. at BERNAVILLE. No1 Sec Cable on line to 11th R.I. Rgt at CANDAS completed and Signal Office opened. All Sections – nothing to report.	
DOMART en PONTHIEU	16.1.16		H.Q. Sec. One reinforcement from Signal Depot received. Wire on strength and posted to No 3 Sec. Nos 2, 3 + 4 Sec. All lines satisfactory. All Sections – nothing to report.	
DOMART en PONTHIEU	17.1.16		No 1 Sec owing to move of 9th H.Q. Signal Office closed at 12 noon and opened in BERNAVILLE	Removed changement of 30 elm. Lines in cover in experiment sauveged
PONTHIEU	18.1.16		at same hour. Signal Office at DOMART handed over to Sig 14th Corps Communication. Linesmen return again to their own D.E. Beadreau and No 9 Pole on S.S. Set 15 line Beulange mattless Sapper thorn D.A. cable of 71265 SS W. elecke and no 71592 3° R.H.	
			Sectn thanks 26 return strength and handed over to No 2 Corps Sig into for duty. No 2 + 4 Secs. Nothing to report.	
BERNAVILLE	19.1.16		No 3 Sec Owing to move of 121st Sig & R.S. Office in BERNAVILLE closed at 12 noon and open in DEMESMONT at same hour.	
			H.Q. No 1 Sec Command as usual Post in S.O. in morning. There was by 14 Corps. Work of fitting up Telephone in H.Q. Corps Office continues. Communications satisfactory but slight contratts between 108 + 109 Re-wired.	

1577 Wt. W10791/1773 500,000 1/15 D. D. & L. A.D.S.S./Forms/C. 2118.

Army Form C. 2118.

36th Div Signal Co "R.E."

WAR DIARY
or
INTELLIGENCE SUMMARY.

(Erase heading not required.)

Instructions regarding War Diaries and Intelligence Summaries are contained in F. S. Regs., Part II. and the Staff Manual respectively. Title pages will be prepared in manuscript.

Place	Date	Hour	Summary of Events and Information	Remarks and references to Appendices
			Nos 1, 2 + 3 Secs Communications satisfactory	Lines dropped
			No 4 Sec Difficulty in touch to AUTHEUX to establish communication with 9th R Inniskg Fus	commenced
BERNAVILLE	20.1.16		H.Q. & No 1 Sec. 105th & 109th Bdes have still no contact and reports when both have nothing practically unintelligible	non military news
			Contact delayed. Contact due to wind, there being no name poles	
			Nos 2 and 3 Secs. Satisfactory.	namezeo
			No 4 Sec 9th R Inniss Fus moved from FIENVILLERS to AUTHEUX - knocked yesterday	appendix 2
BERNAVILLE	21.1.16		H.Q. & Nos 1, 2 + 3 Secs. Nothing to report	
			No 4 Sec Telephone line to Divisional Train faulty due to shortage of magneto ringing Telephones and owing to work on D.III. & difficulty in getting ringing to hear being no tell and no induction	
BERNAVILLE	22.1.16		H.Q. & No 1 & 2 + 3 Secs Nothing to report	
			No 4 Sec Two men from 13th Corps Signals reported their unit	
BERNAVILLE	23.1.16		H.Q. & No 1 Section. 12 men (from 36.) Our Artillery fired for 2 weeks on route of battalion	
			Nos 2, 3, and 4 Secs. nothing to report	
BERNAVILLE	24.1.16		H.Q. & No 1 Sec. Slight contact on 105th and 109th Bde wires probably caused by Wt lines being part of the way on the same poles and dampness	
			Nos 2, 3, and 4 Secs. Nothing to report	

36th Div Signal Co'y R.E.

WAR DIARY
or
INTELLIGENCE SUMMARY
(Erase heading not required.)

Army Form C. 2118

Place	Date	Hour	Summary of Events and Information	Remarks and references to Appendices
BERNAVILLE	25.1.16		H.Q. Nos 1,2 + 3 Secs Communications satisfactory - 36th Div. Arty moved to CAYEUX on 24th taking 2 motor Cyclist Corporals with them, from this hut. Communication with their H.Q. arranged through ABBEVILLE Signal Office. No 4 Sec. Nothing to report.	
BERNAVILLE	26.1.16		H.Q. & No 1 Sec. Contact on 14th Corps Circuit + also on Divisional Area - Cleared by 14th Corps Signals Contact and induction on 108 - 109th Bde. Telephone Circuits - very pronounced - No 1 Section commenced work on Comic Air line to communicate direct with 12th Bde. at AILLY le HAUT CLOCHER H.Q & No 1 Sec. 15 circuit communication established to 12th Bde. at AILLY le HAUT CLOCHER, formerly through 14th Corps Signals at DOMART. Single current set-affects from 14th Corps office. Communication opened with D III Telephone but owing to line being on permanent poles, is severe induction, telephone only used pending S.C. Set becoming available Nos 2 + 3 Secs No report. No 4 Sec. Comic Air line laid to 9th R.I. mon. Two Trestle experienced with contacts on 109th Bde and 109 - 12 Bde Circuits	Circuit Diagram No 2 sent annexed appendices
BERNAVILLE	28.1.16		H.Q. & No 1 Sec on 14th Corps and 109th - 14th Corps taking up line insulators failed Communication uninterrupted but not suspended - Normally resumed at 10 am on completion repairs by 14th Corps. Sounder set now connected on this Circuit.	

1875 Wt. W593/826 1,000,000 4/15 T.R.C. & A. A.D.S.S./Forms/C. 2118.

36th Signal Co 4 R.E.

WAR DIARY
or
INTELLIGENCE SUMMARY
(Erase heading not required.)

Army Form C. 2118

Place	Date	Hour	Summary of Events and Information	Remarks and references to Appendices
BERNAVILLE	29.1.16		No 2 & 4 Sections - nothing to report. No 3 Section. Communication opened with 108th Bde Machine Gun Company at RIBEAUCOURT. H.Q. & No 1 Sec. 108th and 109th Bde. wires intermittently in contact - Contact cleared but communication unsatisfactory. Nos 2 & 3 Secs. lines working satisfactorily.	Circuit diagram J108 Zero =
BERNAVILLE	30.1.16		No 4 Sec. D1 Cable line to AUTHEUX reeled up. H.Q. + Nos 1, 2, & 3 Secs. nothing to report. No 4 Sec. 9th R. Irish Div. moved from AUTHEUX to CANDAS and Signal Office at Railhead CANDAS closed same hour.	Appendices No 4
BERNAVILLE	31.1.16		H.Q. & No 1 Sec. 108th and 109th Bde wires again slightly in contact - 108th Bde. morse circuit dis. for annexes. Left an hour in afternoon. Faults repaired and communication satisfactorily resumed. No 2 Sec. 11 Q 12th Bde. wires 15 45th Bde. Signal Office closed down - 2 men from No 1 Sec. will assist instruments recalled. No 3 Sec. nothing to report. No 4 Sec. 9th R. Irish Div. two more from CANDAS to AUTHEUX. Signal Office closed at 3.30 p.m. and opened at AUTHEUX at 2 p.m. Signal Office of 11/4th (K.O.) Hants Reg. moved into CANDAS and opened at 7.15 p.m. Trench Telephone fitted in Office of R.T.O. CANDAS at 10 a.m.	Circuit diagram 169 0210 line Appendices No 5

31 . 1 . 16

C. A. Reaboro Major
A/36th. DIV. SIG. COY. R.E.

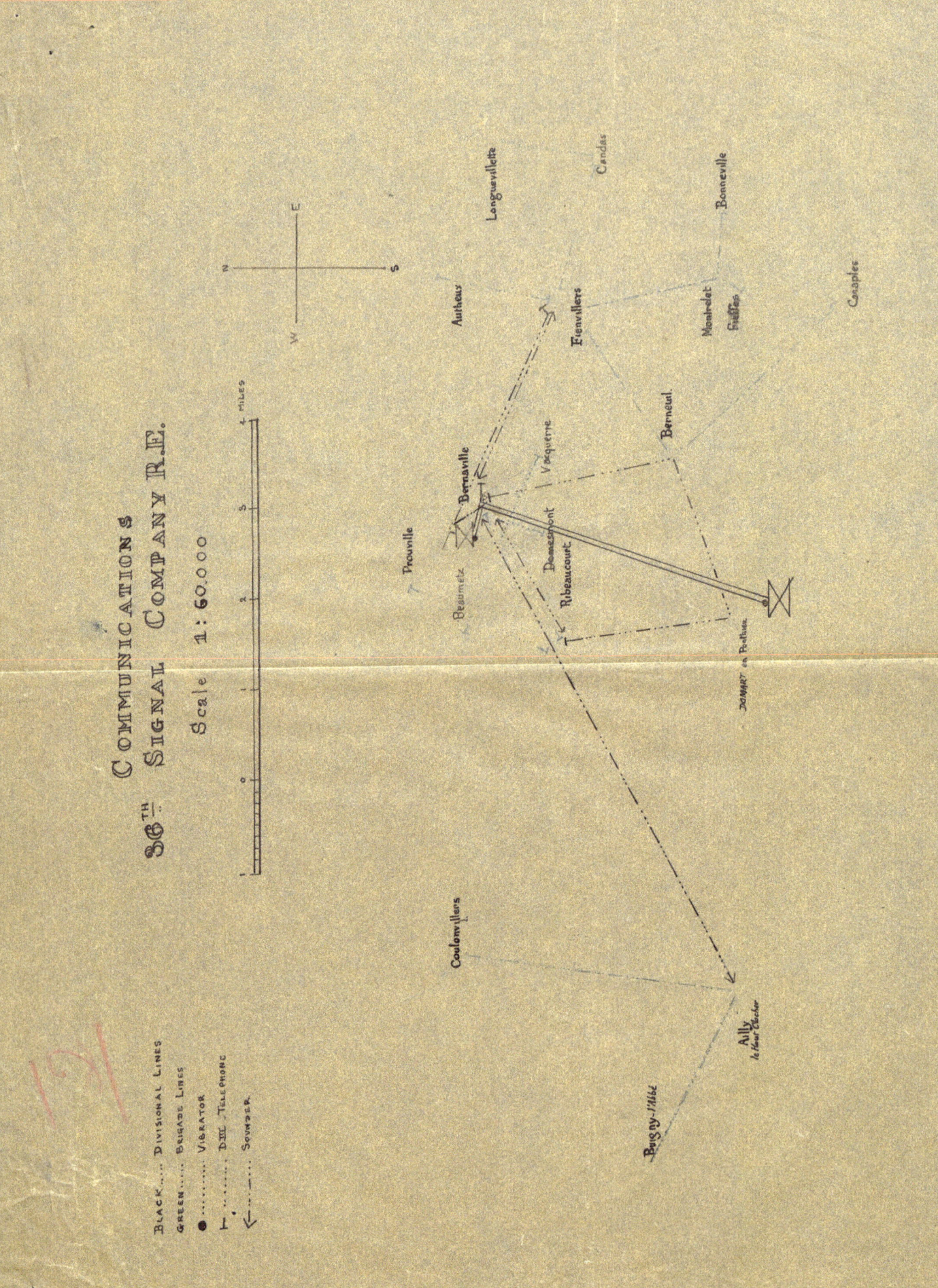

Communications ~ 30th Division Sigs

- Comic ....
- Airline —.—.—
- Cable Dy —..—..—
- Permanent Line ———

Le Meillard

Beauville

Bienvillers N9

Ribeaucourt

N3A N3B

Domart

N7

Canaples

St Ouen

Circuit Diagram LJT 29/1/16.

Scale 1:80000

~~Annexe Sht 12~~

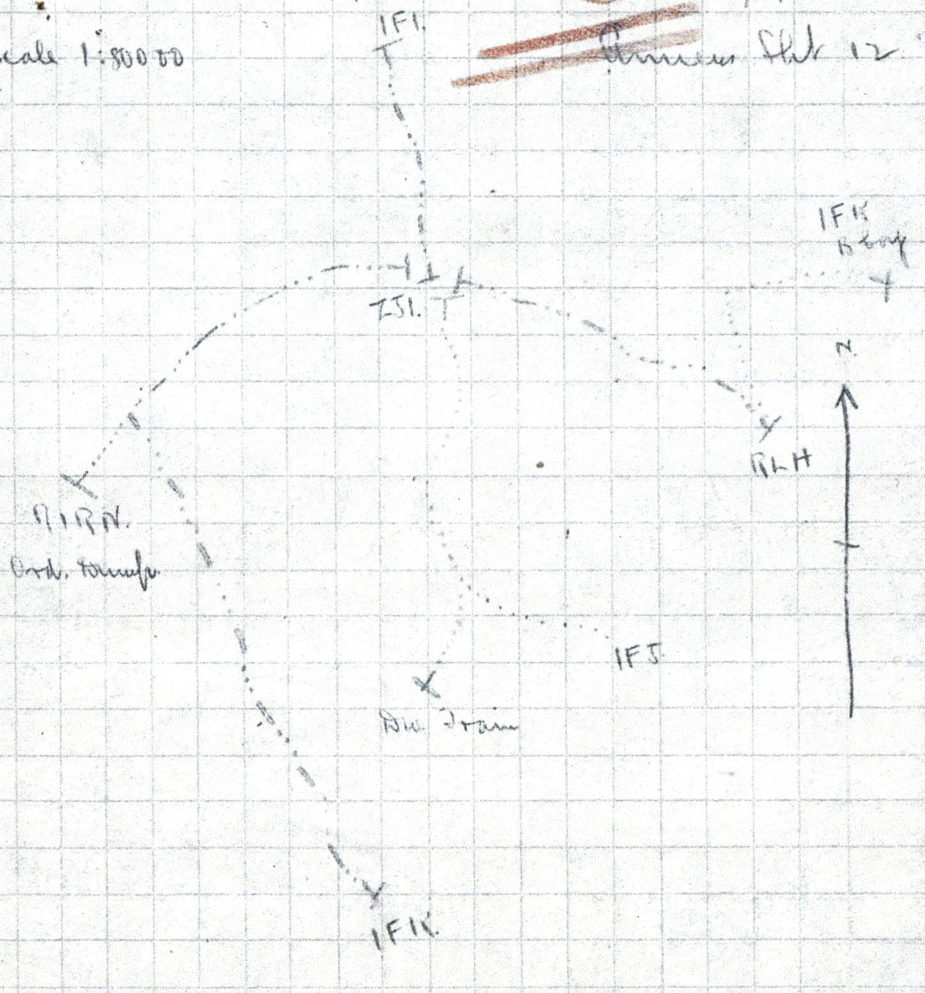

Telephone D III on all lines
except Div Train. (French phone)

29/1/16

W.S. Healy Lt. RE
O.C. Signals

SCALE 1:40,000

COULONVILLERS

Office

BUSSUS-BUSSUS
M¹⁴ de BUSSUS

Office

BUIGNY-L'ABBÉ

ALLIEU

AILLY-
le-HAUT-CLOCHER

Office

36th Div Sig Co
R.E.

Vol 5.

36th (Ulster) Div. Sig. Co. R.E.

Army Form C. 2118

WAR DIARY
or
INTELLIGENCE SUMMARY
(Erase heading not required.)

Instructions regarding War Diaries and Intelligence Summaries are contained in F. S. Regs., Part II. and the Staff Manual respectively. Title Pages will be prepared in manuscript.

Place	Date	Hour	Summary of Events and Information	Remarks and references to Appendices
BERNAVILLE	1.2.16		H.Q. and No. 1 Sec. Command of his Division taken over by 17th Corps. Two men of 14th Corps with Bartrand returned to their Corps and 2 new from 17th Corps with Bartrand reported for duty.	
do	2.2.16		No. 2 and 3 Sections — Nothing to report. No. 4 Section — Trench Telephone at Div. Railhead dismantled — message passing thro' 1/4 (S.O.) Line Regt. H.Q. and No. 1 Sec. Division ordered to move up and occupy position in line occupied by 4th Div. 107th Bde. transferred to this Div. and 12th Bde. to 4th Div. The 107th Bde. to remain in its present position in front line — 108th Bde. to occupy position on its right — 109th Bde. to remain in Reserve. The 108th Bde. commences its march to new area — to establish offices at MARTINSART. Circuit diagram of lines received from 4th Div. also march programme from H.Q. 36th Div. No. 2 Sec. — In future No. 2 Sec. will man the 107th Bde. Signal Section whenever it appears in line control of him away. No. 3 Sec. Bde. Sig. Office closed at 8.30 a.m. and march to new area commenced — 9 R.In. Bns. Offrs also closed down — 53rd Div. R.A., 11th, 12th and 13th R.In. Reg. brigaded into one Div. wire — No. 1 Sec personnel and instruments availed to Co. H.Q.	
do	3.2.16		H.Q. Section. Telephone circuits dismounted at 12 noon and all instruments recalled. Switchboard dismantled — lines led on to Commutator and worked with Telephones Portable D Mk. 3. Div. ripples to all circuits other than Corps circuit worked on D.5 Boardboard — 11th R.In. Reg. commenced march and Officer closed — 4.2.16 H.Q. See Communication Arrangements — 13th R.In. Reg. also dismantled. Advance Parties sent by Rail and lorry to take over 4th Div. Offices at ACHEUX (Div. H.Q. Office), BERNUSSART (Exchange and Testing at R.A. lines) MAILLY-MAILLET (Div. Report Centre and 107th Bde. Office) Party B henceman (mounted) sent by road. Necessary instruments also despatched. Party to be rationed by 4th Div. Sig. Co. up to and including 6th inst. Two Despatch Riders sent to report to 107th Bde. for duty	
do	4.2.16			

Army Form C. 2118

36th Div. Signal Co. R.E. WAR DIARY or INTELLIGENCE SUMMARY

Instructions regarding War Diaries and Intelligence Summaries are contained in F.S. Regs., Part II. and the Staff Manual respectively. Title Pages will be prepared in manuscript.

(Erase heading not required.)

Place	Date	Hour	Summary of Events and Information	Remarks and references to Appendices
BERNAVILLE	4. 3.2.16		No 1 Section. All Telephone wires used up in order to recover cable. 8 miles D5 cable and 6 miles G1. Cable handed over to 4th Div. Signal Co., all existing lines to be taken over from them. No 2, 3 and 4 Sections – no report	
– do –	5. 4.2.16		H.Q. Section – H.Q. 109th Bde and 9th and 10th R. Irish. Fus. with Bde. Machine Gun Section commenced. Communications to remaining 2 Bns. two Bde. Signal Offices (the Rear Party) maintained. Nos 1, 2 and 3 Sections – nothing to report	
– do –	6.2.16		No 4 Section – Signal Offices 115 9th and 10th R. Irish. Fus. closed down. H.Q. Section – Relief for Advance Party sent to 4th Div. Sig. Coy. to carry on office until arrival of remainder of Coy. Nos 1, 2, 3 and 4 Sections – Communications satisfactory – no report	
ACHEUX	7.2.16		H.Q. Section. Div. Office at BERNAVILLE closed at 12 noon, and opened same hour at ACHEUX. Communications taken over from 4th Div. Sig. Coy. Transfer of instruments already made in H.Q. and other offices. Circuits as follows: – H.Q. 15 line metallic Switchboard giving communication to H.Q. Div. Office 107th, 108th and 109th Bdes 17th Corps &c. D.C. Baseboard to 17th Corps S.C. Switch gets to 107th & 108th Bdes Vibrators to Div R.A. worked through Pyramid Exchange in order to embrace all units. In BEAUSSART Office. 10 line Exchange for Telephone working. In MAILLY MAILLET Office. This is the Div. Report Centre and Battle H.Q. – Ten line M/C Switchboard and Vibrator as spare in circuit. Communications satisfactory. One Reinforcement St O. MARTIN taken on strength. Nos 1 and 2 Secs. nothing to report. No 3 Sec. Reports for change on which Bde was on the march :–	Diagrams of Telegraph and Telephone Communications appendixed "A"

1875 Wt. W593/826 1,000,000 4/15 I.B.C. & A. A.D.S.S./Forms/C. 2118.

36th Div. Signal Co. R.E. 3

Army Form C. 2118

WAR DIARY
or
INTELLIGENCE SUMMARY
(Erase heading not required.)

Instructions regarding War Diaries and Intelligence Summaries are contained in F.S. Regs., Part II. and the Staff Manual respectively. Title Pages will be prepared in manuscript.

Place	Date	Hour	Summary of Events and Information	Remarks and references to Appendices
	2.2.16		Signal Stories with 121st Fd. Coy., 108th Fd. Amb., 9th R.I. Sus. and 108th Bde. H.Q. closed. March commenced - Halt in CANAPLES for the night - Office opened, communication by Orderlies	
	3.2.16		Marched from CANAPLES. Halt at TOUTENCOURT for night - Office opened. Communication by Orderlies.	
	4.2.16		Marched from TOUTENCOURT to MARTINSART - H.Q. established at latter place - office taken over from 11th Infy Bde.	
	5.2.16		Office taken over from 11th Bde. Communication established with 11th R.I. Rif. in Trenches, 2nd Q.I.R. and 11th Bde. Machine Gun Co., 9th R.I. Bn. in Trenches (right section), Bde. on right flank, 13th R.I. Rif. and 27th Siege Battery at MESNIL, 15th Bn. Hants Regt. at BEAUVILLE, 1st Bn. Hants Regt. in Trenches (left section) and 15th S.T. Bde. R.F.A. at MARTINSART	
			No 4 Section - Bde. H.Q. established at ACHEUX, his Bde. being in reserve. Communication opened with Bde. Machine Gun Co. at VARENNES, 9th R. Innis. Sus. at BEAUSSART, 10th R. Innis. Sus. at ACHEUX and 122nd Fd. & 84 at FORCEVILLE.	
ACHEUX	8.2.16		H.Q., No. 1 & 2 Secs. Nothing to report. Communications satisfactory. No 3. Sec. Communications satisfactory. No H. Sec. D1 Cable from 15 9th R.I. Innis. Sus. via BERTRANCOURT rolled up. Communication established on enamelled wire line laid beside Railway.	
- do -	9.2.16		H.Q. Sec. Communications Satisfactory - 6 Cyclists attached for duty. In connection with Carrier Pigeon Service administered by his Sig. D.R. sent with relief of Pigeons to Bde. lofts at MARTINSART and MAILLY MAILLET - Telephone installed in O.C.'s residence or Prison. Telephone Casualty report from Section for the closing 24 hours. Nil.	

1875 Wt. W593/826 1,000,000 4/15 T.B.C. & A. A.D.S.S./Forms/C. 2118.

36th Div Signal Co. R.E.

Army Form C. 2118

WAR DIARY
or
INTELLIGENCE SUMMARY
(Erase heading not required.)

Instructions regarding War Diaries and Intelligence Summaries are contained in F.S. Regs., Part II. and the Staff Manual respectively. Title Pages will be prepared in manuscript.

Place	Date	Hour	Summary of Events and Information	Remarks and references to Appendices
ACHEUX	10.2.16		No 1 Sec. On move of 4th Div. Arm. Col. from TOUTENCOURT to ARQUEVES additional communication established to same at 9.45 pm. No 2 and 3 Secs. nothing to report. No 4 Sec. 11th R.I. Innis. Fus. and 14th R.I. Rif. arrived FORCEVILLE and VARENNES respectively. Both tied in on ACHEUX - FORCEVILLE - VARENNES line. H.Q. Sec. 48th Div. reel up wire connecting 108th Div. with 12th Bde. hut now necessary owing to move of 12th Bde. to COLINCAMPS - 6 men received from 36th Cyclist Coy. for duty. No 2 or 3 Secs. nothing to report. No 4 Sec. 109th Bde. Machine Gun Coy. move from VARENNES to MAILLY. Office closed at VARENNES at 10 a.m. 2 men from 10th R.I. Innis. Fus. reported for duty as Pigeon Flyers in connection Carrier Pigeon Service.	
ACHEUX	11.2.16		H.Q. Sec. horse circuit to 17th Corps in contact at 5.20 pm. lineman sent at, communication being maintained on Telephone Circuit. Telephone and wire superimposed through Transformer on Telephone Circuit at 7.20 pm. Fault cleared and normal communication resumed at 9 a.m. No 2,3 and 4 Secs. nothing to report.	
- do -	12.2.16		H.Q. Sec. horse circuit to 108th Bde. earth at 4.45 pm. repaired at 7.30 pm. No 2 Sec. nothing to report. No 3 Sec. Bde. H.Q. move from MARTINSART to ENGLEBELMER - Office closed at MARTINSART at 3 pm. and opened at ENGLEBELMER at same hour. No 4 Sec. 109th Bde. H.Q. move from ACHEUX to MAILLY-MAILLET - Office closed at ACHEUX at 9 a.m. and opened same hour at MAILLY-MAILLET. Communication opened from	

3 b" Div. Signal Co" 4" R E

Army Form C. 2118

WAR DIARY
or
INTELLIGENCE SUMMARY
(Erase heading not required.)

Place	Date	Hour	Summary of Events and Information	Remarks and references to Appendices
ACHEUX	13.2.16		New Office with 9th, 10th and 11th R Irish Fus., 14th R.I. Regt., 107 Bde and 2nd Div R.a. H.Q. + no I Sec. Communications satisfactory – nos 2, 3 + 4 Sec. no report	
– do –	14.2.16		H.Q. Sec. Communication on all lines satisfactory – At 11.35 p.m. Communication (phone) with 7th and 17th corps interrupted – All work phoned – Boardwork and connections overhauled but fault not found. Summary of work transacted – relieving number of messages to deal with during day:- A. messages 187, B. messages 108, C. messages 169, C. messages 169, B.L.S. Appx 167, 131, B. Forms 110, C. Forms 145, B.R.L.S. 240. 15 men from 36th Div. only who were attached to this Coy for instruction returned to their Brigade on completion of course. No I Sec. Engaged on burying lines. nos 2, 3 and 4 Secs. nothing to report	
– do –	15.2.16		H.Q. Sec. Linesman sent out on Corps line as work on more cable and private wire circuit apparatus on Telephone wire Transformer and work continued – Three Ericsson and 4 Tom eln Telephones received to complete new establishment – One Trench Telephone issued to each 107 and 106th Bde as increase on their establishment. Abstract of messages as dealt with. A group	
– do –	16.2.16		H.Q. Sec. Line to 4 Div Ammn Col. dis. at 8 am. Repaired by 11 am. – Wires working on Corps circuit reversed on line being repaired – Relay adjustment on YCF instrument YCF – R20. circuit out of order between 11.10 p.m. and 11.33 p.m.	

36th Div. Signal Co. R.E.

Army Form C. 2118

WAR DIARY
or
INTELLIGENCE SUMMARY
(Erase heading not required.)

Instructions regarding War Diaries and Intelligence Summaries are contained in F.S. Regs., Part II. and the Staff Manual respectively. Title Pages will be prepared in manuscript.

Place	Date	Hour	Summary of Events and Information	Remarks and references to Appendices
ACHEUX	17.2.16		No 1 Sec. Work on burying lines continued.	
			Nos 2, 3 and 4 Secs. nothing to report. Lines satisfactory.	
	18.2.16		H.Q. Sec. Unable to get tho' to 21st Hussars and 127th Bde R.F.A. through BEAUSSART Exchange at 8.30 am. Working subsequently satisfactory. Line to 7th and 17th Corps cut at 8.25 pm. Working resumed - a most unsatisfactory event.	
			Nos 1, 2, 3 and 4 Secs. Communications satisfactory.	
			H.Q. Sec. Communications satisfactory. Particulars of move of 36th Div. R.A. into Div area received. Moves will commence on 25th. Summary of day's work. A. Messages 161 B messages 84	
			C message 169 D.R.L.S. 329	
			Nos 1, 2, 3 & 4 Secs. Nothing to report	
-do-	19.2.16		H.Q. Sec. Communication satisfactory. Summary of work. A message 207 B messages 124	
			C messages 182 D.R.L.S. 345. Very heavy shelling heard at 5 pm. lasting about 1 hour. Reports received that some front line communications damaged by shell fire and were being repaired.	
			Nos 1, 2, 3 & 4 Sections - no report	
-do-	20.2.16		H.Q. Sec. 108th and 109th Bde lines in contact from 12 noon to 12.30 pm. Contact cleared partially but more or less intermittent on lines all the day. Signals not interfered with. Finally cleared abstract of day's working - A message 158 B messages 136 C message 198 D.R.L.S. 398. No 57842 C.Q.M.S. Shelton D.T. Struck off on transfer to Army Printing Shalford Signal Depot.	
			No 1 Section - working on lines	

36th Div. Signal Co. R.E.

Army Form C. 2118

WAR DIARY
or
INTELLIGENCE SUMMARY
(Erase heading not required.)

Instructions regarding War Diaries and Intelligence Summaries are contained in F.S. Regs., Part II. and the Staff Manual respectively. Title Pages will be prepared in manuscript.

Place	Date	Hour	Summary of Events and Information	Remarks and references to Appendices
ACHEUX	21.2.15		Nos 2, 3 + 4 Sections - nothing to report.	
			H.Q. + No 1 Section. Circuit to C.C.O. and R.E.O. dis. at 9.50 a.m. to 10.5 a.m. Fault cleared by Corps and working resumed. There was a considerable amount of work on Corps circuit owing to 2 Corps working in same circuit. An accumulation of work always takes place in the evenings. The 48th Div. Signals have avoided this by accepting some of the messages on their circuit. This means 2½ an mornings but nevertheless saves a good deal of delay. A system which would overcome the difficulty, but this is not to be had.	
ACHEUX	22.2.15		Nos 2, 3 + 4 Sections - Lines all working satisfactorily.	
			H.Q. Section - Communications working well. The D.R.L.S. is increasing - # 37 is the number sent today.	
			A messages 135, B messages 130, C messages 154.	
			No 1 Section - Engaged on lines.	
			Nos 2, 3 and 4 Section - nothing to report.	
ACHEUX	23.2.15		H.Q. + No 1 Section. All communication good. A messages 153, B messages 124, C messages 171. Telephone calls 228, D.R.L.S. 390. Heavy snow fell today but no interference with lines experienced.	
			No 1 and 2 Section - nothing to report	
			No 3 Section - New line completed to night Battalion of Section.	
			No 4 Section - Owing to 109th Bde. relieving 107th Bde. in the Trenches Personnel sent to Report Centre and advanced Battle Head Quarters of 107th Bde. to receive instruction in the working of these Stations.	
ACHEUX	24.2.15		H.Q. and No 1 Section. All of communication with Divisional Ammunition Column from 11 p.m. to 6 p.m. Fault found in their office and cleared. Lieut V.A.C. Cary reported for duty with the Company. Abstract of day's work. A messages 165, B messages 164, C messages 175, D.R.L.S. 427, Telephone Calls 228.	Diagram of 109th Circuits appendix B
			No 2 Section - 107th Bde. relieved in Trenches by 109th Bde. All communications handed over.	

3rd Div. Signal Co. R.E.

Army Form C. 2118

WAR DIARY
or
INTELLIGENCE SUMMARY
(Erase heading not required.)

Instructions regarding War Diaries and Intelligence Summaries are contained in F. S. Regs., Part II. and the Staff Manual respectively. Title Pages will be prepared in manuscript.

Place	Date	Hour	Summary of Events and Information	Remarks and references to Appendices
ACHEUX	25.2.16		No 3 Section – Shindural improvement to Signal Office carried out in Brigade Report Centre. No 4 Section – Connected up No 5 Air line to Report Centre and opened up direct communication with 8th R.In. Rif. at 2pm. Previous communication obtained through 107th Bde. Headquarters Section – Communications satisfactory – Abstract of work A heneages 153, B heneages 166 Cheneage 132 D.R.L.S. 440 Tel. calls 219. No 1 Section – Engaged in burying lines &c No 2 Section – Nothing to report No 3 Section – Trench line buried line to Bde Signal Office from outside ENGLEBELMER completed No 4 Section – Nothing to report	
ACHEUX	26.2.16		H.Q. & No1 Sec. Communications satisfactory – Heavy snowfall all day but no interference with lines No 2 Section – No report No 3 Section – Line buried from Battalion in rest to Bde. Signal Office No 4 Section – Overhauling wires	
ACHEUX	27.2.16		H.Q. Section. Communications Satisfaction – Improvement in communications required – more line require to be buried. Application made for working parties – Abstract of work A heneages 145. B heneages 136 C heneages 194 – D.R.L.S. 355. No 1 Sec. Authes move about to take place. Wiring Office at LOUVENCOURT and preparing for move – move subsequently cancelled. No 2 Sec. Working on Sounder to Div Commenced at 6 pm. No 3 Sec. Completed a metallic circuit between Bde Report Centre and Bns in Trenches No 4 Sec. Overhauling wires	

1875 Wt. W593/826 1,000,000 4/15 J.B.C. & A. A.D.S.S./Forms/C. 2118.

36th Div. Signal Co. 4 R.E.

Army Form C. 2118

WAR DIARY
or
INTELLIGENCE SUMMARY
(Erase heading not required.)

Instructions regarding War Diaries and Intelligence Summaries are contained in F.S. Regs., Part II. and the Staff Manual respectively. Title Pages will be prepared in manuscript.

Place	Date	Hour	Summary of Events and Information	Remarks and references to Appendices
ACHEUX	28.2.16		H.Q. Sec. Communications satisfactory. "Thaw" men also sent out as all Motor Lorry Traffic suspended.	
			No 1 Section - lines working satisfactory	
			No 2 Section - Overhauling lines	
			No 3 Section - Nothing to report - all lines satisfactory	
			No 4 Section - Overhauling lines. Half buried cable repaired	
ACHEUX	29.2.16		H.Q. Section - 108 R.de. Sie. dis. from 11.15 to 11.35. Wire broken down. Repaired - Men from Infantry Bns. were sent in for Testing, which was carried out by Lt. DONNELLY. Coy are now satisfactory.	
			No 2 Section - 8th R.I. Rgt. moved to MAILLY - Communication established.	
			No 3 Section - Nothing to report	
			No 4 Section - New line from Battle H.Q. tested in to old lines and some buried cables replaced.	

In the field
29.2.16.

A.A. Poulton Major
O.C. 36th Div. Sig. Coy R.E.

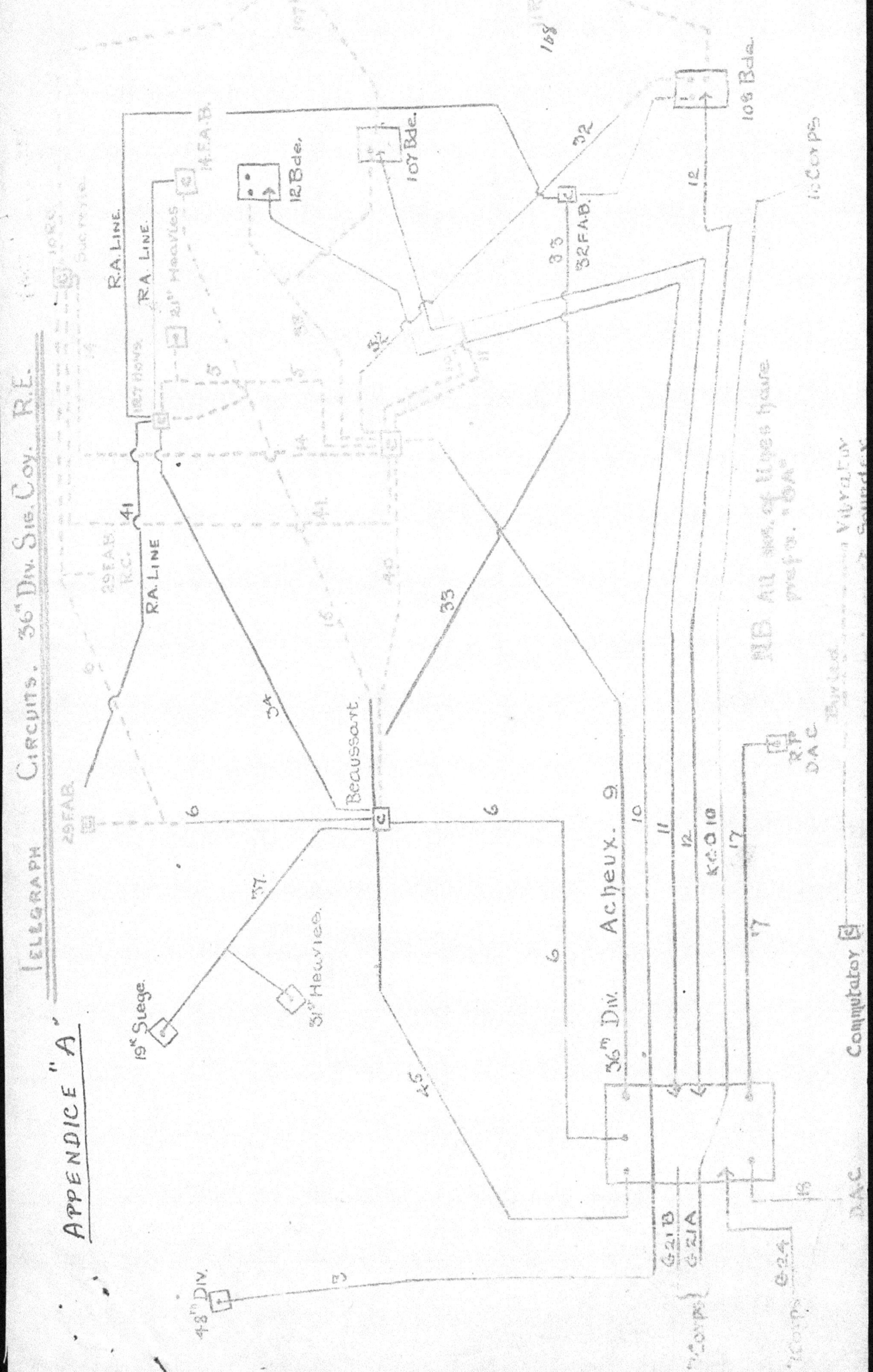

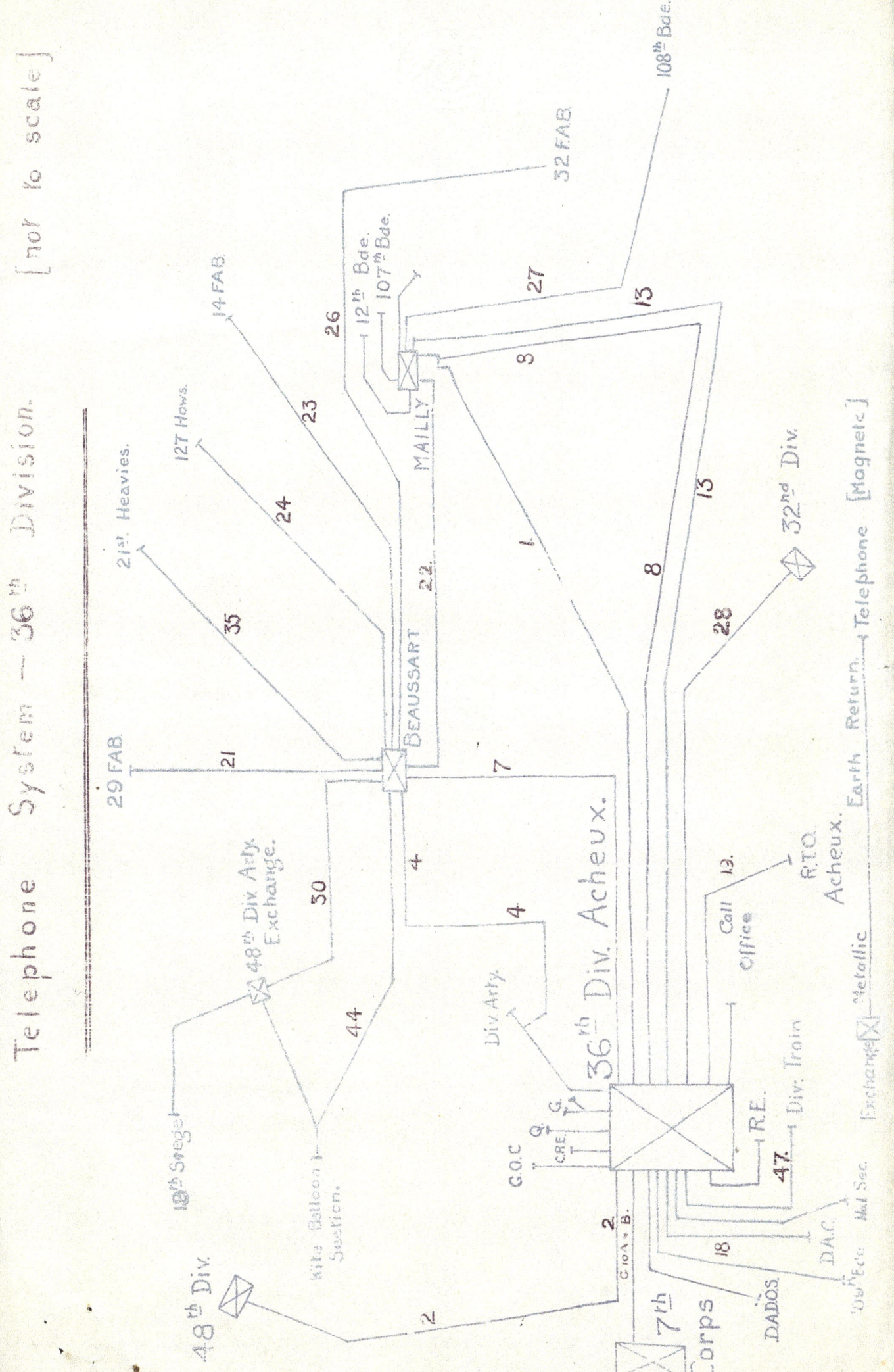

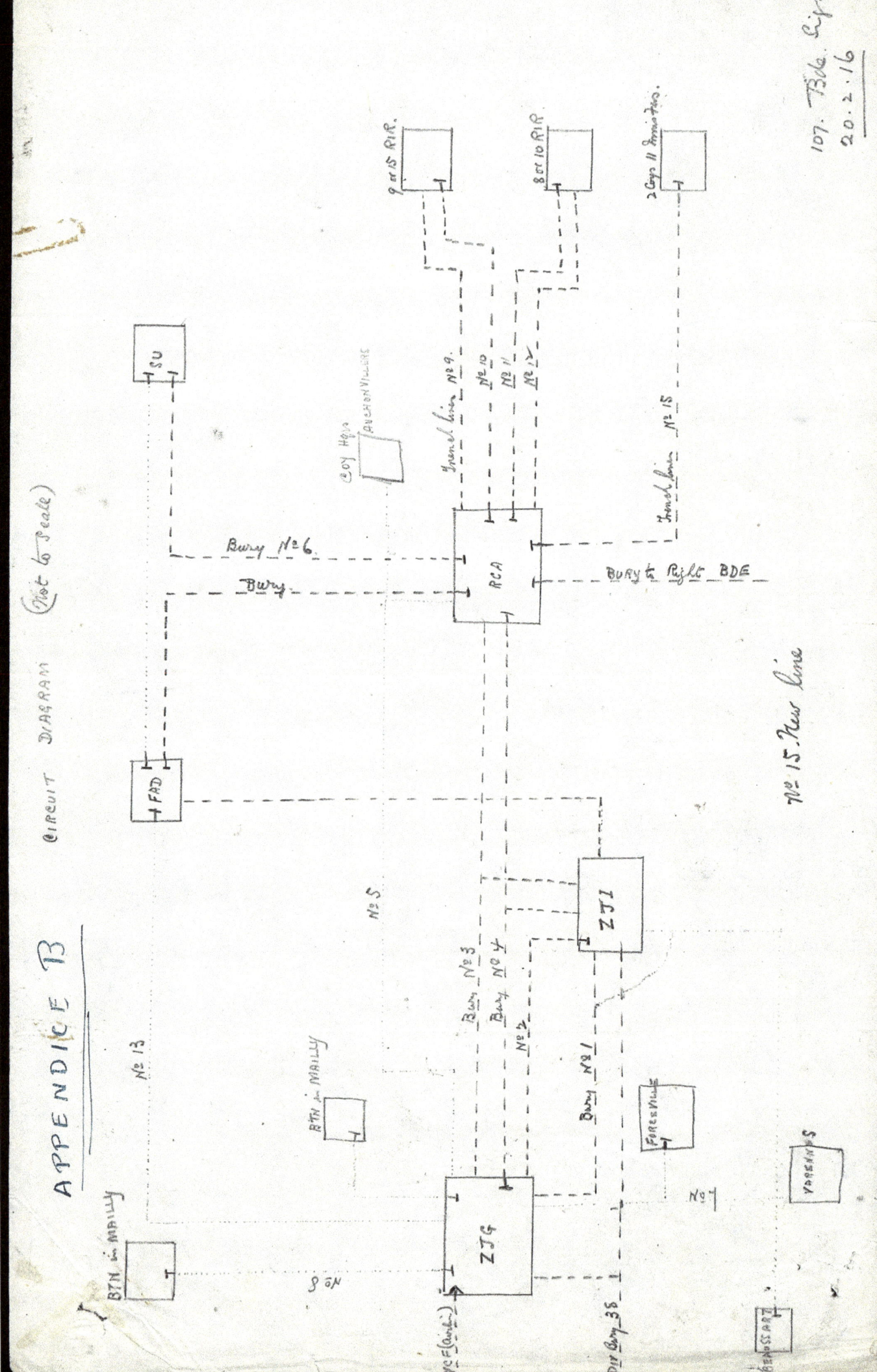

CONFIDENTIAL   36 D. Signals Vol 6

WAR DIARY

— OF —

36th DIVISIONAL SIGNAL COMPANY, R.E

1st MARCH, 1916 ÷ TO ÷ 31st MARCH, 1916

VOLUME .... SIX.

36th Div. Signal Co. 4.R.E.

WAR DIARY or **INTELLIGENCE SUMMARY**
(Erase heading not required.)

Army Form C. 2118

Place	Date	Hour	Summary of Events and Information	Remarks and references to Appendices
ACHEUX	1:3:16		H.Q. and No 1 Sec. 36th Div. Artillery commenced taking over from 4th Div. Arty today - All existing taken over by him - 36th Div. transferred from 17th Corps 3rd Army to 10th Corps 4th Army - The 10th Corps attached 2 Operators and 1 linesman to his unit for duty - Communication with 10th Corps established on Single current set on line formerly running from G.C. to KCO - Headtaken from Pole outside Office - Ringing Telephone put on forward portion of line toward Toutencourt (H.Q. 6th Corps) which 10th Corps eventually take over. Nos 2, 3 & 4 Sections - Communications satisfactory - no other report	
	2:3:16		H.Q. Sec. 4 No 1 Sec. Orders received that 36th Div. to take over additional part of front line - the 107th Bde to relieve the 109th Bde. in Left sector - the 109th Bde taking over front from 146th and 147th Bdes. Then H.Q. 15 be at MARTINSART. All existing communications to be taken over. Nos 2, 3 & 4 Sections - lines all working satisfactorily	
ACHEUX	3:3:16		H.Q. & No 1 Section - H.Q. 107th Bde move from ACHEUX to MAILLY - 109th Bde move from MAILLY to ACHEUX - A new 2nd Intelligence filled up in Office, in place of Pyramid board for Artillery lines. YCF - RCO lie dis from 9.12 am to 9.45 am. No 2 Sec. Bde H.Q. moved from ACHEUX to MAILLY. Communications taken over from 109th Bde, who move to ACHEUX. No 3 Sec. A portion of the 107th Bde Trenches taken over by 108th Bde. No 4th R.Ir. Fus. carry him portion of the sector. Communication established between him and 108th Bde. No 4 Sec. Bde H.Q. moved to ACHEUX.	
ACHEUX	4:3:16		H.Q. & No 1 Sec. New orders of Battle of the Division is as follows:- 107th Bde. assigned 109th Bde. in left sector - The 109th Bde. relieved the 146th and 147th Bdes. on night of the 4th march and established their H.Q. at MARTINSART - The 108th Bde. takes up trenches 51 to 57 from 107th Bde. The 36th Div. Arty. complete him relief of 4th Div. Arty, who leave the area	

2

Army Form C. 2118

36th Div. Signal Coy. R.E.

WAR DIARY
or
INTELLIGENCE SUMMARY
(Erase heading not required.)

Instructions regarding War Diaries and Intelligence Summaries are contained in F.S. Regs., Part II. and the Staff Manual respectively. Title Pages will be prepared in manuscript.

Place	Date	Hour	Summary of Events and Information	Remarks and references to Appendices
ACHEUX	4.3.16		No 2 Sec. ⎫ No 3 Sec. ⎬ Communications satisfactory - nothing unusual to report No 4 Sec. ⎭	
ACHEUX	5.3.16		H.Q. & No 1 Sec. Communication with new 109th Bde H.Q. at MARTINSART established. There was a very heavy fall of snow today and in consequence some difficulty was experienced by lines breaking down, making earths and contacts. Linesmen out all day. Communications not greatly affected with. At about 4 p.m. today enemy dropped H.E. Shells near ACHEUX WOOD - no damage done - no lines broken. No 2 Section - Overhauling lines and routine work No 3 Section - Line laid to 122nd Fld. Coy. R.E. and communication opened at 10 a.m. Line laid from HEDAUVILLE to ENGLEBELMER. Geo line from ENGLEBELMER to new left sector repaired and communication opened. Metallic Circuit to present right sector completed and also a similar line complete to entire sector. No 4 Section - 11th R.I. Innis. from 10th & 11th Bdes. Signal before in MARTINSART taken over from 146th Bde. Communications satisfactory - H.Q. Campbelli move to MARTINSART	
ACHEUX	6.3.16		H.Q. & No 1 Sec. 147th Infy. Bde. relieved by 109th Bde. H.Q. established at ACHEUX. Communication by Telephone, Operators and Linesmen of 17th Corps rejoined their unit. One detachment No 5796 Sapper C.M. COOPER received from Signal Depot and posted to No 1 Section. Communications satisfactory - No 1 Section working on lines. Total work dealt with 989 messages and letters. No 2 Section - Lines laid from 9 to 10 to left half Bn. Our last night by shell fire, repaired immediately	

1875 Wt. W593/826 1,000,000 4/15 J.B.C. & A. A.D.S.S./Forms/C. 2118.

WAR DIARY or **INTELLIGENCE SUMMARY**

Army Form C. 2118

36th Div Signal Coy R.E.

Place	Date	Hour	Summary of Events and Information	Remarks and references to Appendices
ACHEUX	7.3.16		No 3 Section - line from HEDAUVILLE to ENGLEBELMER completed. This makes communication with Batteries in Brigade Reserve. Brigade right Sector in trenches handed over to 109 Bde. Signal Office in MESNIL to 14th R.Ir. Rif.	
			No 4 Section. Completed taking over from 147th Bde. at 2.30 p.m. Communication to Trenches and right and left Brigades satisfactory. Two lines to Report Centre cut by Shell fire and repaired.	
			H.Q. and No 1 Section. Communications satisfactory - newspapers and letters dealt with... 972	
			No 2 Section - Routine - Repairs to lines	
			No 3 Section - Metallic circuit to left Sector completed - Enemy aeroplane dropped Bomb in ENGLEBELMER - No damage	
			No 4 Section - Took over 1st and 2nd West Riding Bdes R.F.A and 10th Hvy Bde R.F.A from 147th Inf. Bde. Relied up 10th Hvy Bde line during the morning. 153rd Bde R.F.A took over from 1st W. Riding Bde. Communications to relieving unit opened. Have line to 106th Bde Report Centre to connect with line to HAMEL and MESNIL in rear of this Brigade taking over part of 108th Bde. Sector - Reliefs in this Sector completed 8.30 p.m. Communications satisfactory. Messages A - 50, B - 10, C - 50, Total 150	
ACHEUX	8.3.16		H.Q. & No 1 Section - Communications good - new line laid from MARTINSART to MAILLY For change to connect up 163rd Bde R.F.A with Div. R.A. Headquarters	
			No 2 Section - Nothing to report	
			No 3 Section - Heavy Artillery Bombardment between 7p.m. and 8 p.m. Work on lines in left Section continued. Communications good and not interfered with by Bombardment.	
			No 4 Section - new line to MESNIL and HAMEL Road. All communications satisfactory - No. of Messages - 154	

36th Div. Signal Coy. R.E.

Army Form C. 2118

WAR DIARY or INTELLIGENCE SUMMARY

(Erase heading not required.)

Place	Date	Hour	Summary of Events and Information	Remarks and references to Appendices
ACHEUX	9.3.16		H.Q. + No 1 Section - All communications good. Two reinforcements (Drivers Pine and Morrison) received from Signal Depot and taken on strength. Total hansaps 802 - Telephone Calls 281. No 2 Section - no report. No 3 Section - New line from Report Centre to Left Section completed - Commenced burying line from Left Section to Report centre and Bde. Headquarters. No 4 Section - New buried earths dug for Brigade Office - new 15 line Switchboard provided by Brigade Staff installed - Air line to MESNIL and HAMEL not satisfactory having been broken several times.	
ACHEUX	10.3.16		H.Q. Section + No 1 Section. Communications Satisfactory. Aerial buried D6 Cable buried 7 days ago, tested and found satisfactory - no appreciable loss of current register. No 2 Section - no report. No 3 Section - Communications Satisfactory. No 4 Section - Intellix Circuit laid 15.12.15 by Field Coy. R.E. to MARTINSART and connected to Telephone Switchboard. Found to connect up Town Commandant, Pithy Patrol + Enemy Instructed Right Section from 11 p.m. to midnight. Two Brigade Section wires broken down. Communication maintained. Artillery communications with Battalions broke down completely and has to be maintained through Brigade Signal Offices. No. of Messages 178.	
ACHEUX	11.3.16		H.Q. and No 1 Section. Telephone connection made with 74 R.E. Park ACHEUX and Army Heavy Artillery Group - Both lines laid by Corps Signals. Messages 1012. Telephone Calls 252. No 2 Section. No report. No 3 Section - New line from Left Section to Bde. H.Q. partly buried.	

36th Div. Signal Co. R.E.

Army Form C. 2118

WAR DIARY
or
INTELLIGENCE SUMMARY
(Erase heading not required.)

Place	Date	Hour	Summary of Events and Information	Remarks and references to Appendices
ACHEUX	12.3.16		No 4 Section - 14th R/Ir Rif relieved 11th R/Innis Fus in trenches - Communications handed over.	
			H.Q. & No 1 Sec. Communications satisfactory - No of messages 8, 14. Telephone Calls 201.	
			No 2 Section - No report	
			No 3 Section - new line from left section to Bde H.Q. partly buried	
			No 4 Section - Bn. on line Z.2 and Y.3 repaired - No of messages 143.	
ACHEUX	13.3.16		H.Q. & No 1 Section - In connection on line to 173rd Bde. R.F.A. from 3pm to 8.18pm - houses unknown but on this line	
			No 2 Section - Communications satisfactory	
			No 3 Section - line from H.Q. to 27th Siege Battery repaired and communication opened. line from left section to H.Q. partly buried.	
			No 4 Section - Ringing Telephone on direct spare line established to GORDON CASTLE and connected to switchboard giving direct telephone communication to right Bn H.Q. Rump Teals make - not satisfactory	
ACHEUX	14.3.16		H.Q. Section & No 1 Communication satisfactory	
			No 2 Section - Overhead direct line to left Bde.	
			No 3 Section - line to left section partly buried. Burying of old line completed	
			No 4 Section - Trench or metallic circuit from GORDON CASTLE to report centre commenced. Small progress made owing to exposed position and artillery bombardment. Lamp signalling from GORDON CASTLE to report centre completed. Patrol found several lengths or last copper wire in NO MANS LAND suspended from barbed wire stakes to one of our caps. Attempt at taking wire	

36th Signal Coy. R.E.

Army Form C. 2118

WAR DIARY
or
INTELLIGENCE SUMMARY
(Erase heading not required.)

Instructions regarding War Diaries and Intelligence Summaries are contained in F.S. Regs., Part II. and the Staff Manual respectively. Title Pages will be prepared in manuscript.

Place	Date	Hour	Summary of Events and Information	Remarks and references to Appendices
ACHEUX	15.3.16		Inspected Bombardment of enemy position opposite THIEPVAL WOOD carried out in slight retaliation. One line cut.	
			H.Q. & No 1 Section - Communications satisfactory	
			No 2 Section - no report.	
			No 3 Section - Burying of line from left sector to Bde. H.Q. proceeding	
			No 4 Section - Labelling of lines in Right Section completed	
ACHEUX	16.3.16		H.Q. Section - General. One Officer and 2 D.O.R. T&H Cable Section arrived and attached to Company for work in this area - for reeling up of spare used lines	
			No 2 Section - Line to left Bde partly cut out and replaced by new D 5 Cable - One man wounded by Rifle fire	
			No 3 Section - Line from Bde. H.Q. to report centre dis from 5.5 pm to 6.30 pm. Communication maintained on spare line	
			No 4 Section - New line or "B" Satellite cable laid along HAMEL road from Report Centre to left Bn. H.Q. in HAMEL. Line pegged in Trenches	
ACHEUX	17.3.16		H.Q. Section - Communications satisfactory. To horses in addition to establishment received as Chargers for hunt CLERY.	
			No 1 Section - Working on Air line to MESNIL.	
			No 2 Section - Communications satisfactory.	
			No 3 Section - Plough used in breaking up ground for Trench for buried line to report centre	
			No 4 Section - Works on burying lines progressing	

Army Form C. 2118

36th Div. Signal Co. R.E.

WAR DIARY
or
INTELLIGENCE SUMMARY
(Erase heading not required.)

Instructions regarding War Diaries and Intelligence Summaries are contained in F. S. Regs, Part II. and the Staff Manual respectively. Title Pages will be prepared in manuscript.

Place	Date	Hour	Summary of Events and Information	Remarks and references to Appendices
ACHEUX	18.3.16		H.Q. Section – 2nd Lieut Armytage R.E. joined the Company today – attached to assist and for instruction. Communications satisfactory.	
			No 1 Section – working on lines	
			No 2 Section – nothing to report	
			No 2 Section – work on buried lines continued	
			No 4 Section – Complete metallic circuit from GORDONS CASTLE to Report Centre – Some dead cable picked up	
ACHEUX	19.3.16		H.Q. Section – Communications working satisfactorily	
			No 1 Section – working on air lines from HEDAUVILLE to MESNIL. Communication satisfactory	
			No 2 Section –	
			No 3 Section – Work on burying lines continued – One line from Bde. H.Q. to Report Centre cut by enemy Artillery	
			No 4 Section – Work on buried lines continued. Trench relief carried out	
ACHEUX	20.3.16		H.Q. Circuit to 109th Bde. din from Stan. 15 to 6 p.m. – Line broken and repaired. Communication kept up through 153rd Bde. R.E.O.	
			No 1 Section – working on air lines – 10 Comic lines being run out from HEDAUVILLE towards MESNIL	
			No 2 Section – Communications satisfactory	
			No 3 Section – work on buried line continued	
			No 4 Section – Still working on burying lines. Some dead cable recovered	
ACHEUX	21.3.16		H.Q. Section – All lines working well – No Message dealt with – 904.	
			No 1 Section – working on lines in the MESNIL area	
			No 2 Section – communications good	
			No 3 Section – Work on buried lines in left Section continues – Enemy artillery active – no interference with current	

8

3 (?) Div. Signal Co. R.E.

WAR DIARY
or
INTELLIGENCE SUMMARY
(Erase heading not required.)

Army Form C. 2118

Place	Date	Hour	Summary of Events and Information	Remarks and references to Appendices
ACHEUX	22.3.16		No 4 Section - Trench for new metallic circuit from Report Centre to HAMEL commenced - work on cabling huts continued - Trench relief carried out - messages dealt with - 106. H.Q. and No 1 Section - Party of 2 officers and 10 W.O.s from 3/1st Gloucester 19— Signal Coy attached in connection with taking over - 2nd Lieut. Ormandy reported for duty. Messages dealt with A - 163, B. 93, C - 169. Telephone calls 232 - D.R.L.S. 431. No 2 Section - Communications satisfactory No 3 Section - new line from Bde. H.Q. to report centre completed - work on buried lines in left sector continued - One officer and 3 W.E.s from party attached from 3/1st Gloucester Section No 4 Section - Direct Telephone communication with Bn. in HAMEL established on spare lines. 2nd Lieut. ARMYTAGE reported for duty. No of messages 106.	
ACHEUX	23.3.16		H.Q. + No 1 Section - heavy batteries but on circuit from H.Q. to 107th Bde - 3.20 p.m. to 4.20 p.m. owing to slight intermittent contact on Corps circuit - cleared - No of messages A - 117, B - 82, C - 137 - D.R.L.S. - 384 Telephone Calls 174 No 2 Section - Line to FORCEVILLE and BEAUSSART broken by snow - Repaired. No 3 Section - New buried line from Bde. H.Q. to left Section completed No 4 Section - line from Report Centre to HAMEL commenced from earth return to metallic circuit. Messages dealt with 147	
ACHEUX	24.3.16		H.Q. Section - Tests made with carrier pigeons during preceding week gave satisfactory results - only one bird failing to reach its destination. No 1 Section - Lieut. Donnelly working in MARTINSART area to assist artillery in recovering dead lines and improving their communications.	

Army Form C. 2118

36th Divisional Signal Co. R.E.

WAR DIARY or INTELLIGENCE SUMMARY
(Erase heading not required.)

Instructions regarding War Diaries and Intelligence Summaries are contained in F.S. Regs., Part II. and the Staff Manual respectively. Title Pages will be prepared in manuscript.

Place	Date	Hour	Summary of Events and Information	Remarks and references to Appendices
ACHEUX	25.3.16		No 2 Section – lines to BEAUSSART and FORCEVILLE again broken by snow during night. Repaired by 9 a.m. I Officer and 4 O.R. of 31st Div. inspected the inspection of lines. No 3 Section – Communications satisfactory. No 4 Section – Further progress made with new trench from Bde. Report Centre to H.A. Communication established. Wires from H.Q. to 57th Seige Battery to & messages 216. H.Q. and No 1 Section. Party from 31st Div. Signal Co. 4 to return on 26th. Communications good. No of messages A150 B80 C178 D.R.L.S. 373 Telephone calls 203. No 2 Section – No 10 line to left sector broken 8 pm. Repaired immediately. Communications good. No 3 Section – Communications satisfactory – messages dealt with A44 B26 C26. No 4 Section – Burying of cable to Report Centre continued. To left Sub Section Rn. Reg. Officers reports that it is impracticable to bury lines from Rn. to Co H.A. owing to subsoil. Trench is to be passing through ruined village – only alternative is to bury an extension to existing trenches - No messages 122.	
ACHEUX	26.3.16		H.Q. & No 1 Sec. Party from 31st Div. left today to rejoin their unit. Communications satisfactory. No of messages: A79 B72 C177 D.R.L.S. 373 Tel. calls 225. No 2 Section. Lieut. Lindsay proceeded on leave. Lieut. Cherry took over the Section. Working party engaged in laying additional line to Right Bn. – Lamp tests successfully carried out. No 3 Section. Party from 31st Div. left to rejoin their unit. Lines working well. No 4 Section – Burying cable continued. Communications good. No of messages 138.	
~~ACHEUX~~	~~27.3.16~~			
ACHEUX	27.3.16		A.D. Section. Information received that Div. H.Q. to move to HARPONVILLE but nothing definite at	

Army Form C. 2118

36th Divisional Signal Co. R.E.

WAR DIARY
or
INTELLIGENCE SUMMARY
(Erase heading not required.)

Instructions regarding War Diaries and Intelligence Summaries are contained in F.S. Regs, Part II. and the Staff Manual respectively. Title Pages will be prepared in manuscript.

Place	Date	Hour	Summary of Events and Information	Remarks and references to Appendices
ACHEUX	28.3.16		present: No 1 Section - no report No 2 Section - no report No 3 Section - Relief of 108th Bde. by 92nd Inf. Bde. commenced - (13th R. Ir. Rifles moved to FOREEVILLE. Office handed over to 10th East Yorks - Some new lines required) No 4 Section - Work on buried lines continued - Trench reliefs carried out - Communications satisfactory.	
			H.Q. & No 1 Section - Arrangements made for relief of left and centre Brigades by 3 (P) Division. Relief commenced on 27th in centre section by relief of 13th R. Ir. Rif. No 2 Section - Line to right sub-sector converted into metallic circuit. Line to FORCEVILLE appears - heavy test carried out. No 3 Section - New line laid from HEDAUVILLE to FORCEVILLE and VARENNES. 2 Coys 9 R. Ir. Rif. Fus. moved to MESNIL - No 2 Sec. (92nd Inf. Bde.) 31st Divn arrived and arrangements made for handing over. No 4 Section - Work on buried lines continued. Telephone communication established with 150 Field Coy. R.E.	
ACHEUX	29.3.16		H.Q. & No 1 Sec. 2nd Lieut DODDS reported for duty vice Lieut. CLERY transferred to 32nd Divn Sig. No 2 Section - 93rd Bde. Signal Section arrived for taking over area - line to 31st Divn connected up through Y.C.F. (36th Divn) No 3 Section - Bde Signal Office handed over to 92nd Bde. Signals - Bde. H.Q. transferred to VARENNES. Office opened at VARENNES at 11am. No 4 Section - Work on buried lines continued - Communication satisfactory	

Army Form C. 2118

36th Div. Signal Co. R.E.

WAR DIARY
or
INTELLIGENCE SUMMARY
(Erase heading not required.)

Instructions regarding War Diaries and Intelligence Summaries are contained in F.S. Regs., Part II. and the Staff Manual respectively. Title Pages will be prepared in manuscript.

Place	Date	Hour	Summary of Events and Information	Remarks and references to Appendices
ACHEUX	30.3.16		H.Q. & No 1 Section - Lines Satisfactory. No 2 Section - Nothing to report. No 3 Section - Line to Division poled - Work on line to FOREEVILLE continued. No 4 Section - Still Burying lines	
ACHEUX	31.3.16		H.Q. & No 1 Section - Communications satisfactory - Sounder set put on 108th Bde line in place of D III Telephone. Out of direct communication with 107th Bde, owing to them moving out of the line. No 2 Section - Office handed over to 93rd Bde Signals - Bde. H.Q. moved to PUCHEVILLERS. Communication with Division through Army and Corps H.Q.'s. No 3 Section - Work on line to FOREEVILLE completed. Section engaged in transit signalling work. No 4 Section - Work on burying Cable continued - Trench relief carried out.	

In the field
31.3.16

C.A. Preston Major

O.C. 36th Div. Sig. Coy. R.E.

CONFIDENTIAL.

War Diary

of

36th Divisional Signal Company. R.E.

FROM

1st APRIL, 1916

TO

30th APRIL, 1916.

Nihilities .... THE SIXTH.

SECRET

CFS/320

Officer i/c
    Adjutant General's Office.
        at the Base.

    Herewith Volume Six War Diary of this Unit, please, covering period from 1st April 1916, to 30th April, 1916.

                      Captain R.E.
        O.C. 36th Divisional Signal Coy,.R.E.

In the Field.
3 = 6 = 16.

Army Form C. 2118.

WAR DIARY
or
INTELLIGENCE SUMMARY.
(Erase heading not required.)

Instructions regarding War Diaries and Intelligence Summaries are contained in F. S. Regs., Part II. and the Staff Manual respectively. Title pages will be prepared in manuscript.

Place	Date	Hour	Summary of Events and Information	Remarks and references to Appendices
ACHEUX	1.4.16		One cable Detachment to HEDAUVILLE to be attached to Div Arty for work. Strength 1 Offr. 35 O.R.	
"	2.4.16		Nothing to report	
"	3.4.16		29th Div relieved 36th Div & handed over Div Signal Office and lines to 36th Div Signal Coy. 36 Div Sig moved to HARPONVILLE. Signal Office opened there — Lines laid by No 1 Section. Lieut Armytage transferred to 32 Div Signal Coy. Left for that Unit	
HARPONVILLE	4/4/16		Nothing to report	
"	5/4/16		Lieut V. N. G. Lilley O.B.E transferred to 32nd Div Sig Coy. Left O.R.E Depot	
	6/4/16		Nothing to report	
	7/4/16		Nothing to report	
	8/4/16		Telephone circuit - Corrie Avuluer - to 108 Bde built	
	9/4/16		Nothing to report	
	10/4/16		Nothing to report	
	11/4/16		108 Bde move to MARTINSART and take over trenches. Communication established	

Army Form C. 2118.

WAR DIARY
or
INTELLIGENCE SUMMARY.
(Erase heading not required.)

Instructions regarding War Diaries and Intelligence Summaries are contained in F. S. Regs., Part II. and the Staff Manual respectively. Title pages will be prepared in manuscript.

Place	Date	Hour	Summary of Events and Information	Remarks and references to Appendices
HARPONVILLE	12/4/16		Nothing to report	
"	13/4/16		Nothing to report	
"	14/4/16		Nothing to report	
"	15/4/16		One reinforcement received and posted to No 4 Section.	
"	16/4/16		Nothing to report	
"	17/4/16		Nothing to report	
"	18/4/16		One reinforcement received posted to No 3 Section.	
"	19/4/16		Nothing to report	
"	20/4/16		Div. HQrs moved to HEDAUVILLE. Signal Officer closed in HARPONVILLE 11.0 AM Opened HEDAUVILLE somehow — no listeners built — Communication to 3 Bde Infantry & 2 Bde Arty Batteries. Burying of wire continued. The sound of hammering wrinkles very well within 2 feet and telephone to rear dugouts. One match put up with this of the wire is to be kept out.	
HEDAUVILLE	21/4/16			
	22/4/16		Nothing to report	
	23/4/16		Nothing to report	

Army Form C. 2118.

WAR DIARY
or
INTELLIGENCE SUMMARY.
(Erase heading not required.)

Instructions regarding War Diaries and Intelligence Summaries are contained in F. S. Regs., Part II. and the Staff Manual respectively. Title pages will be prepared in manuscript.

Place	Date	Hour	Summary of Events and Information	Remarks and references to Appendices
HEDAUVILLE	24/4/16		Nothing to report. Drove to Divisional Report Centre giving trouble with contacts	
"	25/4/16		Major G.A Preston proceeded to Base. Command of Unit taken over by Capt Jnr. Bedgeworth R.E.	
	26/4/16		Nothing to report	
	27/4/16		Nothing to report	
	28/4/16		Nothing to report	
	29/4/16		Nothing to report	
	30/4/16		Nothing to report	

7.5.16

Bedgeworth
Capt RE
O.C. 38A Dn Sig Coy RE

CONFIDENTIAL

War Diary

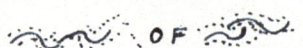
of

36th Divisional Signal Company, R.E.

From

1st May, 1916

to

31st May, 1916.

Volume .... The Eighth.

36 Signals
Vol 8

SECRET.

CFS/372

Officer l/c
    Adjutant General's Office,
        Base.

        Herewith Volume Eight of War Diary of this Unit covering period from 1st to 31st ultimo.

                              Captain R.E.
                    O.C.36th Divisional Signal Coy,.R.E.

In the Field,
6 = 6 = 16.

Army Form C. 2118.

WAR DIARY
INTELLIGENCE SUMMARY.
(Erase heading not required.)

Instructions regarding War Diaries and Intelligence Summaries are contained in F. S. Regs., Part II. and the Staff Manual respectively. Title pages will be prepared in manuscript.

Place	Date	Hour	Summary of Events and Information	Remarks and references to Appendices
HEDAUVILLE	1.5.16		Nothing to report	
"	2.5.16		Heavy Thunderstorm and lightning affected wires. Three coils on Indicators on Telephone & Buzzing fused. Buzzer lines and instruments also affected. Loud noises on all lines	
	3.5.16		Nothing to report	
	4.5.16		Nothing to report	
	5.5.16		Nothing to report	
	6.5.16		Visual Stat between HAMEL and MARTINSAR successfully carried out	
	7.5.16		Trench Relief. 108 Bde relieving over all Divisional front - 109 Bde to Divisional Reserve. Visual working over all communications	
	8.5.16		Nothing to report	
	9.5.16		Nothing to report	
	10.5.16		Nothing to report	
	11.5.16		Nothing to report. 108 Bde Section's morning party stopped and dispersed by shrapnel.	
	12.5.16		Nothing to report	

Army Form C. 2118.

WAR DIARY
or
INTELLIGENCE SUMMARY.
(Erase heading not required.)

Instructions regarding War Diaries and Intelligence Summaries are contained in F.S. Regs., Part II. and the Staff Manual respectively. Title pages will be prepared in manuscript.

Place	Date	Hour	Summary of Events and Information	Remarks and references to Appendices
HEDAUVILLE	13/5/16		Nothing to report.	
	14/5/16		Visual Station on MESNIL Ridge manned.	
	15/5/16		Nothing to report	
	16/5/16		Nothing to report	
	17/5/16		Brigade in not have a field day. Gave them lines and telephones	
	18/5/16		Another field day.	
	19/5/16		Brigade wires maintains communication to its Battalions by Visual Station. Lamps employed at night	
	20/5/16		Brigade wires have another field day. Again provided communication	
	21/5/16		Nothing to report	
	22/5/16		Nothing to report	
	23/5/16		Brigade in rest practice signalling to aeroplanes of Contact Patrol	
	24/5/16		Nothing to report	
	25/5/16		Question of communicating to aircraft again engages attention of Brigade wires. All methods standardised up to present employed. Results much. Reactioned that communication	

1577 Wt. W10791/1773 500,000 1/15 D. D. & L. A.D.S.S./Forms/C. 2118.

Army Form C. 2118.

WAR DIARY
or
INTELLIGENCE SUMMARY.
(*Erase heading not required.*)

Place	Date	Hour	Summary of Events and Information	Remarks and references to Appendices
HEDAUVILLE	27.5.16		Can be made from Hedauville to Aveluy provided Observn has a knowledge of own engineering.	
"	28.5.16		Nothing to report.	
"	29.5.16		Nothing to report.	
"	30.5.16		107th Bde. relieves 108th Bde. Usual handing over of communications.	
"	31.5.16		Nothing to report.	
"			During the period under report the chy work on trenches and the improvemt and carrying out of a scheme of deep dug out communications in the Divisional line. Working parties of 190 men were employed on digging the necessary trenches from 108 to 18 Survers Party were relieved from by parties from 116 & 117 West Yorks Reg to Total strength of New Parties 600 men.	

signature
Capt. R.E.
OC 36th Divl Signal Company R.E.

1.6.16

36th Divisional Engineers

36th DIVISIONAL SIGNAL COMPANY R. E.

JUNE 1916::

SECRET

D.A.G. 3rd Echelon
~~36th Division G.~~

      Herewith War Diary covering period from 1st to 31st ultimo.

                           [signature]

                                   Captain, R.E.
      O.C. 36th Divisional Signal Coy,. R.E

9th July, 1916.

Army Form C. 2118

WAR DIARY
INTELLIGENCE SUMMARY
(Erase heading not required.)

36th Div Signal Coy RE

Instructions regarding War Diaries and Intelligence Summaries are contained in F.S. Regs., Part II. and the Staff Manual respectively. Title Pages will be prepared in manuscript.

Place	Date	Hour	Summary of Events and Information	Remarks and references to Appendices
In the Field	1/6/16		Nothing to report	
	2/6/16		Nothing to report	
	3/6/16		Arranged maine communication from PROSPECT POINT to MARTINSART. Overhauled and repaired lines connecting stations.	
	4/6/16		Nothing to report	
	5/6/16		Nothing to report	
	6/6/16		Nothing to report	
	7/6/16		Sent party of One Officer & OR to 4th Squadron R.F.C. for course of instruction on signalling from & reconnoitring aircraft.	
	8/6/16		108th Bde have a field day with 109 Bde. Signalling to contact Patrol Aeroplane carried out.	

Army Form C. 2118

WAR DIARY
or
INTELLIGENCE SUMMARY
(Erase heading not required.)

Instructions regarding War Diaries and Intelligence Summaries are contained in F. S. Regs., Part II. and the Staff Manual respectively. Title Pages will be prepared in manuscript.

Place	Date	Hour	Summary of Events and Information	Remarks and references to Appendices
In the train 9/6/16	9/6/16		nothing to report	
In the train	10/6/16		108 in Bow Field Day. Row section out	
"	11/6/16		nothing to report	
"	12/6/16		nothing to report	
"	13/6/16		nothing to report	
"	14/6/16		nothing to report	
	15/6/16		Wires from Div HQrs Signal Officer to Div Rd. Kwd down and transferred into two rents on high poles Thus doing away with a forest of telephones on the the single route previously existing; and giving the owner of the bum the opportunity of cultivating another acre or two. Had a party from 49th Divnl Signal Coy at this spt.	
	16/6/16		nothing to report	

Army Form C. 2118

WAR DIARY
INTELLIGENCE SUMMARY
(Erase heading not required.)

Instructions regarding War Diaries and Intelligence Summaries are contained in F.S. Regs., Part II. and the Staff Manual respectively. Title Pages will be prepared in manuscript.

Place	Date	Hour	Summary of Events and Information	Remarks and references to Appendices
In the Field	17/6/16		Nothing to report	
"	18/6/16		Nothing to report	
	19/6/16		Nothing to report	
	20/6/16		Party of 25 N.C.O's and men reported and arrived in order that they might be in a position to take over.	
	21/6/16		Nothing to report	
	22/6/16		Nothing to report	
	23/6/16		Changes over Telegraph Offices Divisional Report centre from Armstrong Huts to Dug Out now just ready. Completion of dug out living three months under construction	
	24/6/16		A system of buried communications lines complete	
	25/6/16		Nothing to report	
	26/6/16		Took over and manned station at McMahon's Post and MARTINSART	

Army Form C. 2118

WAR DIARY
or
INTELLIGENCE SUMMARY
(Erase heading not required.)

Instructions regarding War Diaries and Intelligence Summaries are contained in F. S. Regs., Part II. and the Staff Manual respectively. Title Pages will be prepared in manuscript.

Place	Date	Hour	Summary of Events and Information	Remarks and references to Appendices
In the Field	27/6/16		Nothing to report	
	28/6/16		Nothing to report	
	29/6/16		Office at Div Report Centre finally transferred to dug out	
In the Field	30/6/16		Manned Visual Stations on MESNIL Ridge. All preparations for active Operations completed.	

In the Field
1st July 1916

[signature]
Capt RE
O.C. 36th Division Signal Coy. RE

36th SIGNAL COMPANY — 36th DIVISION

36th Divisional Engineers

36th DIVISIONAL SIGNAL COMPANY

JULY 1916 ::

Army Form C. 2118

WAR DIARY
or
INTELLIGENCE SUMMARY
(Erase heading not required.)

36th Div. Sig. Coy. RE Vol II

Place	Date	Hour	Summary of Events and Information	Remarks and references to Appendices
In the Field	1/8/16		Commenced tracing out forward buried system, this was necessary as lines had not been properly cying to the fact that the outgoing Division had only been in the area for a few days, and the previous Division for very little longer.	
	2/8/16		Tested lines forward from Div Report Centre, removing all tees, and burying deeper where required	
	3/8/16		Nothing to report	
	4/8/16		Companies in line put through to their covering batteries	
	5/8/16		Div front extended. 108th Bde Sigs took over from 107 Bde Sigs. 107 Bde Sigs moved into new part of line	
	6/8/16		Nothing to report	
	7/8/16		Continued tracing and putting through Company buried system.	
	8/8/16		Nothing to report	
	9/8/16		Line from Bde Hqrs to Battns. dug up and repaired.	
	10/8/16		Part of dead lines reeled in	
	11/8/16		Nothing to report	

Army Form C. 2118

WAR DIARY
or
INTELLIGENCE SUMMARY
(Erase heading not required.)

36th Div Signal Coy R.E.

Place	Date	Hour	Summary of Events and Information	Remarks and references to Appendices
In the Field	1/7/16		Division assembled under Dummy Offensive Operations. The following were the arrangements made for the Signalling Communications during the Offensive. Cable re-testing trenches feet deep in specially dug trenches, this being run as far as possible to provide alternative means of 'getting through' to any Unit should any one line go dis. All trenches in Cable trenches were metalled - the two legs being twisted together - thus reducing overhearing to a minimum. Test boxes were arranged on all routes. Only in one case did these prove a source of weakness to the system, one box about 1,000ft from the front line being wrecked by a direct hit during the preliminary bombardment. The next put	

WAR DIARY
or
INTELLIGENCE SUMMARY
(Erase heading not required.)

Army Form C. 2118

Place	Date	Hour	Summary of Events and Information	Remarks and references to Appendices
			in the system was the battle in the marshy ground on either side of the River ANCRE. The marsh was about 500 yards wide, and was covered with water, varying in depth up to ten feet. All that could be done was to run a number of 10 ft. cables, and trust in providence. As the enemy's barrage was placed on the marsh these cables were cut again and again by shells. Repairs were always carried out, and with the exception of one line which proved obdurate communication was maintained. The lines to Battalion Headquarters at THIEPVAL WOOD were cut four or five times by one fire, but were repaired, no battalion being cut off for more than 35 minutes. Specially made Metallic Bugger Boards of cable were made Metallic wire all	

WAR DIARY or INTELLIGENCE SUMMARY

Army Form C. 2118

(Erase heading not required.)

Instructions regarding War Diaries and Intelligence Summaries are contained in F.S. Regs., Part II. and the Staff Manual respectively. Title Pages will be prepared in manuscript.

Place	Date	Hour	Summary of Events and Information	Remarks and references to Appendices
			The advance front was also covered by two visual stations to send messages back by, thus on capturing enemy positions. These were not much use as messages were sent back. Wires were also provided but was not much use except in one case for test messages. With the assault three lines per Battalion were laid out. The lines were broken at each halt and ties off again with the advance. One line remained through for twelve minutes — the remainder being cut almost hourly by the enemy's barrage, which, with the assault, was heavy, and no pinpoints or no man's land. The casualties in laying out these wires were heavy. Visual signalling was tried without success. Methods of … … of delivering it impossible to read at	

WAR DIARY
or
INTELLIGENCE SUMMARY

(Erase heading not required.)

Army Form C. 2118

Place	Date	Hour	Summary of Events and Information	Remarks and references to Appendices
	July 2nd		Any distance and casualties amongst the signallers were very heavy. Signallers designated to did not move forward, and communication to Watson Section trenches was maintained by Runner. The Company now very heavy, only nine men wounded - all slightly. On relief of Division in the night communications handed over to Signals of 4th Division. Necessary personnel being left with him to point out routes etc. Divisional HdQrs moved to HEDAUVILLE	
	July 3		Nothing to report	
	" 4		Nothing to report	

Army Form C. 2118

WAR DIARY
or
INTELLIGENCE SUMMARY

(Erase heading not required.)

Instructions regarding War Diaries and Intelligence Summaries are contained in F.S. Regs., Part II. and the Staff Manual respectively. Title Pages will be prepared in manuscript.

Place	Date	Hour	Summary of Events and Information	Remarks and references to Appendices
	July 5		Divisional Headquarters moved to RUBEMPRE.	
	" 6		Nothing to report	
	" 7		Nothing to report	
	" 8		Nothing to report. Prepared to move off on 9th	
	" 9		Divisional Headquarters moved - by MarchRoute - to BERNAVILLE. Communication to Reserve army arranged through Test station in town	
	"			
	10th		Nothing to report	
	11th		Nothing to report	
	12th		moved to FREVANT by MarchRoute. Arrangements for Reserve Army seen. Detained at STEINBECQUE STEINBECQUE. Ballooned Headquarters at BLARINGHAM.	
	13th		Divisional Headquarters moved to TILQUES. Company Returned parties arranged Circuits moved by Road	

1875 Wt. W593/826 1,000,000 4/15 J.B.C. & A. A.D.S.S./Forms/C. 2118.

WAR DIARY
or
INTELLIGENCE SUMMARY

(Erase heading not required.)

Army Form C. 2118

Place	Date	Hour	Summary of Events and Information	Remarks and references to Appendices
	July 14		Moved to ST. OMER and Recomm[enced] army.	
	" 15		Nothing to report	
	" 16		Nothing to report	
	" 17		Nothing to report	
	" 18		Divisional Artillery commenced arriving in area on withdrawal from line	
	" 19		Divisional Artillery H.Q. established arrangements made for connecting them up	
	" 20		Royal School exercises at POLINCOVE now in marching order. 150 Visions arrived from Battalions being trained	
	" 21		Divisional H.Q. moved to ESQUELBECQ	

WAR DIARY
or
INTELLIGENCE SUMMARY

(Erase heading not required.)

Army Form C. 2118

Instructions regarding War Diaries and Intelligence Summaries are contained in F. S. Regs., Part II. and the Staff Manual respectively. Title Pages will be prepared in manuscript.

Place	Date	Hour	Summary of Events and Information	Remarks and references to Appendices
	July 22		nothing to report	
	" 23		Drummie Coys moved to MONT NOIR. Infantry took over line again. move by Motor Route	
	24		nothing to report	
	25		nothing to report	
	26		Arrangements now to ship Drummie Engines School by Motor Bus to BAILLEUL on 27th	
	27th		nothing to report	
	28th		nothing to report	
	29th		nothing to report	
	30th		nothing to report { In the Field }	
	31st		nothing to report	

M Welworth
Capt RE
OC 36th Div Drummie Coy RE

Army Form C. 2118

WAR DIARY
or
INTELLIGENCE SUMMARY
(Erase heading not required.)

36th Div Sig Coy RE

Instructions regarding War Diaries and Intelligence Summaries are contained in F. S. Regs., Part II. and the Staff Manual respectively. Title Pages will be prepared in manuscript.

Place	Date	Hour	Summary of Events and Information	Remarks and references to Appendices
In the Field	12/8/16		Nothing to report	
"	13/8/16		Nothing to report	
"	14/8/16		Nothing to report	
"	15/8/16		Work at sorting out and repairing lines proceeded with	
"	16/8/16		Nothing to report	
"	17/8/16		Nothing to report	
"	18/8/16		Screening buzzers established at intervals along front line to prevent overhearing in Telephone lines	
"	19/8/16		Nothing to report	
"	20/8/16		Nothing to report	
"	21/8/16		Nothing to report	
"	22/8/16		Owing to the unsatisfactory state of buried lines in wet weather a trench Airline scheme commenced.	
"	23/8/16		Nothing to report	
"	24/8/16		Nothing to report	
"	25/8/16		Nothing to report	
"	26/8/16		Nothing to report	
"	27/8/16		All Screening Buzzers reported working satisfactorily	
"	28/8/16		Nothing to report	
"	29/8/16		Nothing to report	
"	30/8/16		Nothing to report	
"	31/8/16		Nothing to report	

Commanding 36th Signal Company R.E.

Army Form C 2118.

Vol 2

36th Div Sig Coy R.E.

WAR DIARY
or
INTELLIGENCE SUMMARY
(Erase heading not required.)

Instructions regarding War Diaries and Intelligence Summaries are contained in F.S. Regs., Part II. and the Staff Manual respectively. Title Pages will be prepared in manuscript.

Place	Date	Hour	Summary of Events and Information	Remarks and references to Appendices
In the field	1/9/16		Div Hqrs moved from Mont Noir to St Jans Cappel. Signal office at Mont Noir closed at 2 PM and opened at St Jans Cappel at 5 PM. Two offices were necessary, one at L Branch who were in chateau some distance from Village, this office was in direct communication by Telegraph with Corps Bdes, Report Centre and with Telephone exchange office, the Telephone exchange office was in St Jans Cappel and was in direct communication by phone with Corps Bdes etc.	
	2/9/16		Communication through to Corps Bdes etc	
	3/9/16		Nothing to report	
	4/9/16		Nothing to report	
	5/9/16		Party from 109 Bde Sigs proceeded to Dranoutre to go over lines of 57 Bde previous to taking them over	
	6/9/16		Nothing to report	
	7/9/16		109 Bde Signals proceeded to Dranoutre and took over office and lines of 57 Bde.	
	8/9/16		Nothing to report	
	9/9/16		Nothing to report	
	10/9/16		Nothing to report	
	11/9/16			

Army Form C. 2118.

WAR DIARY
or
INTELLIGENCE SUMMARY
(Erase heading not required.)

36th Div Sig Coy R.E.

Instructions regarding War Diaries and Intelligence Summaries are contained in F.S. Regs., Part II. and the Staff Manual respectively. Title Pages will be prepared in manuscript.

Place	Date	Hour	Summary of Events and Information	Remarks and references to Appendices
In the Field	12/9/16		Arranged visual stations to work from Bde Hqrs forward	
	13/9/16		Nothing to report	
	14/9/16		Nothing to report	
	15/9/16		Nothing to report	
	16/9/16		Communication by visual opened from Bde Hqrs forward	
	17/9/16		Nothing to report	
	18/9/16		Lack lines connecting up visual stations	
	19/9/16		Nothing to report	
	20/9/16		Nothing to report	
	21/9/16		12th Bde, 4th Canadian Div put through on sounder and phone on coming under command of G.O.C. 36th Div	
	22/9/16		Nothing to report	
	23/9/16		Nothing to report	
	24/9/16		17 Bde & 4th Canadian Div disconnected on leaving Division	
	25/9/16		Nothing to report	
	26/9/16		Nothing to report	
	27/9/16		Nothing to report	
	28/9/16		Nothing to report	
	29/9/16		Nothing to report	
	30/9/16		Nothing to report	

W. Wentworth Capt RE
O.C. 36th Div Sig Coy R.E.

Army Form C. 2118.

Vol 13

WAR DIARY
or
INTELLIGENCE SUMMARY

(Erase heading not required.)

36th Div. Sig. Coy R.E.

Place	Date	Hour	Summary of Events and Information	Remarks and references to Appendices
In the Field	1/X/16		Nothing to report	
"	2/X/16		Nothing to report.	
"	3/X/16		Capt. T.W. Mgono R.E. took over command of Coy. vice Capt. J.A. Edgworth R.E. to X Corps Signal Coy.	
"	4/X/16		Nothing to report	
"	5/X/16		Nothing to report.	
"	6/X/16		Nothing to report.	
"	7/X/16		Nothing to report.	
"	8/X/16		Nothing to report.	
"	9/X/16		2 Lt. J.R. Robartenay - Thomson took over command of No 3 Sect. vice 2 Lt. W. Howe RE to Hqrs. (108th Bde Sect)	
"	10/X/16		Nothing to report.	
"	11/X/16		Nothing to report.	
"	12/X/16		Nothing to report.	
"	13/X/16		Nothing to report.	
"	14/X/16		Nothing to report.	
"	15/X/16		Nothing to report.	
"	16/X/16		Nothing to report.	
"	17/X/16		Nothing to report.	

Army Form C. 2118.

WAR DIARY
or
INTELLIGENCE SUMMARY
(Erase heading not required.)

36th Div Sig Coy R.E.

Instructions regarding War Diaries and Intelligence Summaries are contained in F. S. Regs., Part II. and the Staff Manual respectively. Title Pages will be prepared in manuscript.

Place	Date	Hour	Summary of Events and Information	Remarks and references to Appendices
Intelfield	18/X/16		Nothing to report	
"	19/X/16		Second Class at Div Signal School opened. Artillery Bdes joined the course of Instruction. 120 men from Battalions and	
"	20/X/16		Nothing to report.	
"	21/X/16		Nothing to report.	
"	22/X/16		Nothing to report	
"	23/X/16		Nothing to report	
"	24/X/16		Nothing to report	
"	25/X/16		Nothing to report.	
"	26/X/16		Nothing to report.	
"	27/X/16		Nothing to report	
"	28/X/16		Nothing to report.	
"	29/X/16		Nothing to report.	
"	30/X/16		Nothing to report.	
"	31/X/16		Nothing to report	

J W Wise
Capt RE
OC 36th Div Sig Coy RE

Army Form C. 2118.

WAR DIARY
or
INTELLIGENCE SUMMARY
(Erase heading not required.)

36 J. Div. Sig. Coy R.E.

Vol 14

Instructions regarding War Diaries and Intelligence Summaries are contained in F. S. Regs., Part II. and the Staff Manual respectively. Title Pages will be prepared in manuscript.

Place	Date	Hour	Summary of Events and Information	Remarks and references to Appendices
ในวิธีวิธี	1/11/16		Nothing to report	
"	2/11/16		do	
"	3/11/16		do	
"	4/11/16		do	
"	5/11/16		2/Lt Deutsch R.E. joined for duty on appn transfer from S.R. Supn.	
"	6/11/16		Nothing to report	
"	7/11/16		2/Lt J.S. Collingwood joined for duty on transfer from 2nd Army Signals	
"	8/11/16		Nothing to report	
"	9/11/16		do	
"	10/11/16		do	
"	11/11/16		do	
"	12/11/16		do	
"	13/11/16		do	
"	14/11/16		do	
"	15/11/16		do	
"	16/11/16		2/Lt J.S. Collingwood E. Surrey Regt transferred to 2nd Army	
"	17/11/16		Nothing to report	
"	18/11/16		do	
"	19/11/16		do	

WAR DIARY or INTELLIGENCE SUMMARY

Army Form C. 2118.

36th D.W. Sig. Coy R.E.

Place	Date	Hour	Summary of Events and Information	Remarks and references to Appendices
In the Field	20/1/16		Lieut R.T. Dealey R.E. proceeded to G.H.Q. for a course of instruction at Central Wireless School	
"	21/1/16		Nothing to report	
"	22/1/16		do	
"	23/1/16		do	
"	24/1/16		do	
"	25/1/16		do	
"	26/1/16		do	
"	27/1/16		Lieut R.T. Dealey rejoined on completion of course at Central Wireless School G.H.Q.	
"	28/1/16		Nothing to report	
"	29/1/16		do	
"	30/1/16		do	

J.W.Wilson
O.C. R.E.
Commanding ... Signal Company R.E.

Army Form C. 2118.

WAR DIARY
or
INTELLIGENCE SUMMARY
(Erase heading not required.)

Instructions regarding War Diaries and Intelligence Summaries are contained in F. S. Regs., Part II. and the Staff Manual respectively. Title Pages will be prepared in manuscript.

Vol /5

Place	Date	Hour	Summary of Events and Information	Remarks and references to Appendices
In the Field	1/12/16		Nothing to report	
"	2/12/16		do	
"	3/12/16		do	
"	4/12/16		do	
"	5/12/16		do	
"	6/12/16		109 Inf Bde moved from Bienvillers to reserve at Neuve Église	
"	7/12/16		Nothing to report	
"	8/12/16		do	
"	9/12/16		do	
"	10/12/16		do	
"	11/12/16		do	
"	12/12/16		do	
"	13/12/16		do	
"	14/12/16		do	
"	15/12/16		do	
"	16/12/16		do	
"	17/12/16		do	
"	18/12/16		do	
"	19/12/16		do	

Army Form C. 2118.

WAR DIARY
or
INTELLIGENCE SUMMARY

(Erase heading not required.)

Instructions regarding War Diaries and Intelligence Summaries are contained in F. S. Regs., Part II. and the Staff Manual respectively. Title Pages will be prepared in manuscript.

Place	Date	Hour	Summary of Events and Information	Remarks and references to Appendices
In the Field	20/12/16		Nothing to Report	
"	21/12/16		do	
"	22/12/16		do	
"	23/12/16		do	
"	24/12/16		During the heavy gale a few pair routes and 10 carries routes, leading from Wulverghem Farm, were blown down.	
"	25/12/16		In the afternoon enemy shelled 10 pdr Inf Bde area and in consequence the following lines went out. 1 spare line to GD6 and one spare route to F03 also laterial poled cable routes between Wulvergem and English Farm. These lines & No 2 Section were working.	
"	26/12/16		Nothing to Report	
"	27/12/16		173rd Brigade R.F.A. relieved by 180th Brigade R.F.A. and proceed to Balun Training Area.	
"	28/12/16		do	
"	29/12/16		172 Brigade R.F.A. relieved Batteries of 113th Bde and now covering Right Sector.	
"	30/12/16		Hq 172 Brigade R.F.A. moved from English Farm to Neuve Eglise.	

2449 Wt. W14957/M90 750,000 1/16 J.B.C. & A. Forms/C.2118/12.

Army Form C. 2118.

WAR DIARY
or
INTELLIGENCE SUMMARY
(Erase heading not required.)

Place	Date	Hour	Summary of Events and Information	Remarks and references to Appendices
In the field	29/7/16		Nothing to report	
"	30/7/16		Battalions of 108th Brigade moved to rest on being relieved by Battalions of 109th Inf. Brigade	
"	31/7/16		Nothing to report	

for O.C. 36th Div. Sig. Coy R.E.

Army Form C. 2118.

WAR DIARY
or
INTELLIGENCE SUMMARY
(Erase heading not required.)

36th Signal Coy

Instructions regarding War Diaries and Intelligence Summaries are contained in F. S. Regs., Part II. and the Staff Manual respectively. Title Pages will be prepared in manuscript.

Place	Date	Hour	Summary of Events and Information	Remarks and references to Appendices
In the Field.	1917 Jan 1		Nothing to report	
	2		do.	
	3		do.	
	4		do.	
	5		do.	
	6		do.	
	7		do.	
	8		do.	
	9		do.	
	10		do.	
	11		2/Lt. J. R. Courtenay-Thompson R.E. relinquished Command of 108 Inf. Bde. Signal Section and is transferred to 36th Div. Signals.	
	12		Lt. W. J. Howe, R.E. assumed Command of 108 Inf. Bde. Signal Section.	
	13		Capt: J. E. Lutton, 9th R. S. Fus. joined for duty	
	14		Nothing to report	
	15		do.	
	16		do.	

Army Form C. 2118.

WAR DIARY
or
INTELLIGENCE SUMMARY
(Erase heading not required.)

Instructions regarding War Diaries and Intelligence Summaries are contained in F.S. Regs., Part II. and the Staff Manual respectively. Title Pages will be prepared in manuscript.

Place	Date 1917	Hour	Summary of Events and Information	Remarks and references to Appendices
In the Field	Jan 17		Nothing to report.	
	18		do.	
	19		do.	
	20		do.	
	21		do.	
	22		do.	
	23		do.	
	24		do.	
	25		do.	
	26		do.	
	27		108 Inf. Bde. on relief of 104 Inf Bde. took ov Headqrs at Ga 10	
	28		109 Inf Bde took ov Hdqrs at G.B.7. Signal Office B.B.6 closed down.	
	29		Nothing to report.	
	30		do.	
	31		do.	

Capt. R.E.
for O.C. 36th DIV. SIG. COY R.E.
1/2/17

Army Form C. 2118.

WAR DIARY
INTELLIGENCE SUMMARY
(Erase heading not required.)

36th Div. Signal Coy R.E.

Vol 17

Place	Date	Hour	Summary of Events and Information	Remarks and references to Appendices
In The Field	1/2/17		Nothing to report	
"	2/2/17		do	
"	3/2/17		do	
"	4/2/17		do.	
"	5/2/17		do.	
"	6/2/17		do	
"	7/2/17		do	
"	8/2/17		do	
"	9/2/17		do	
"	10/2/17		do	
"	11/2/17		do	
"	12/2/17		do	
"	13/2/17		do	
"	14/2/17		Visual Test carried out by 108th Bde between Battalions in line and Brigade, which proved satisfactory	
"	15/2/17		T8 visual station opened on Hill 63 and orders issued relating to the working of same	
"	16/2/17		Nothing to report	
"	17/2/17		do	
"	18/2/17		do.	

Army Form C. 2118.

WAR DIARY
or
INTELLIGENCE SUMMARY
(Erase heading not required.)

Instructions regarding War Diaries and Intelligence Summaries are contained in F.S. Regs., Part II. and the Staff Manual respectively. Title Pages will be prepared in manuscript.

Place	Date	Hour	Summary of Events and Information	Remarks and references to Appendices
In the Field	19/2/17		Nothing to report	
"	20/2/17		do	
"	21/2/17		do	
"	22/2/17		172nd Bde. R.F.A moved out of NEUVE-EGLISE. Position taken over by 113th Bde R.F.A.	
"	23/2/17		Nothing to Report	
"	24/2/17		T8 Visual post taken over from 13th R.IR.RIF. by 11th R.IR.RIF	
"	25/2/17		Nothing to Report	
"	26/2/17		109th Brigade moved from English Farm to BAILLEUL, their position being taken over by 107th Bde.	
"	27/2/17		Nothing to report	
"	28/2/17		do.	

for O.C. [signature] /L.R.E.

36th DIV. SIG. COY R.E.
[stamp]

Army Form C. 2118.

WAR DIARY
or
INTELLIGENCE SUMMARY

36th Div. Sig. Coy R.E.

Vol 18

(Erase heading not required.)

Place	Date	Hour	Summary of Events and Information	Remarks and references to Appendices
Zuytpeene	1/3/17		Nothing to Report	
	2/3/17		Working parties arranged with 14th and 13th Rfles Cos for burying cable from Right Coy of Right Battn. to Cable bury at CALGARY AV. to STINKING FARM.	
	3/3/17		11th Royal Ir. Rifles relieved 13th R.I.Rif. in Right Subsector	
	4/3/17		Nothing to Report	
	5/3/17		-do-	
	6/3/17		-do-	
	7/3/17		At 11 p.m. enemy opened intense bombardment on Left Coy of Brigade Front (11 R.Ir.R.). All communication from Bde. Company Head-quarters cut. Call for retaliation was through before wires were cut, and subsequent communication kept up by runner	

Army Form C. 2118.

WAR DIARY
or
INTELLIGENCE SUMMARY 36th Divl. Sig. Coy RE

(Erase heading not required.)

Instructions regarding War Diaries and Intelligence Summaries are contained in F.S. Regs, Part II. and the Staff Manual respectively. Title Pages will be prepared in manuscript.

Place	Date	Hour	Summary of Events and Information	Remarks and references to Appendices
In the Field	8/3/17		At 6 AM enemy again bombed left subsector. All communications stood throughout although FRONT LINE and SERVICE TRENCH were very badly knocked about.	
	9/3/17		Rewiring of Office at FO 2 completed. 30 pr.w. terminal strip put in. All leads at trench to this Office made into route with cleats, cable stakes and corkscrew batterns.	
	10/3/17		Nothing to report	
	11/3/17		Party from Signal section of 2nd New Zealand Bde. arrived as advance party for taking over area. Several p.w.s in stokes cable route from NE 16 A L cut by shell fire and repair. Enemy second circuit lit on AL cement dug-out	
	12/3/17		Right Battalion (108 Bde) took over additional front extending its right to point where New DOUVE crosses FRONT LINE. Communication to additional front worked through exchange at LA PLUS DOUVE FARM.	

Army Form C. 2118.

WAR DIARY
or
INTELLIGENCE SUMMARY 36th Div. Sig. Coy. R.E.

(Erase heading not required.)

Instructions regarding War Diaries and Intelligence Summaries are contained in F.S. Regs., Part II. and the Staff Manual respectively. Title Pages will be prepared in manuscript.

Place	Date	Hour	Summary of Events and Information	Remarks and references to Appendices
In the Field	13/3/17		Left Battalion (108 Bde) extended its left front and took over line to point of junction of WULVERG HEM - WYTSCHAETE ROAD with front line, taking over signal stations FM 5 and F 6.	
	14/3/17		Connections put through from Bde. Signal Office to Battalion Headquarters at LA PLUS DOUVE FM (9D9) and Battalion Hqrs. at RED LODGE (GF4)	
	15/3/17		Brigade Relieved by 2nd New Zealand Bde. Signal Office handed over at 12-noon and opened with new Bde Hqrs. at FLETRE Somme hours connected by telephone to Division	
	16/3/17		Lt. W.T. Williams joined for duty from IX Corps and posted to signals, 107th Brigade.	
	17/3/17		Nothing to Report	
	18/3/17		do	

WAR DIARY or INTELLIGENCE SUMMARY

Army Form C. 2118.

36th Div. Signal Coy R.E.

Place	Date	Hour	Summary of Events and Information	Remarks and references to Appendices
In the Field	19/3/17		Communication arranged between Dunster and DRANOUTRE Exchange	
	20/3/17		109th Bgde HQrs moved to Second Army Funny Circus from BAILLEUL to BOUVELINGHEM. 108th Bde moved to BAILLEUL	BOUVELINGHEM
	21/3/17		Nothing to Report	
	22/3/17		Communication established by Signals 109th Bde between BOUVELINGHEM and ST. OMER	
	23/3/17		Lieut W. T. Williams returned 107th Bde Signals reported in 6.15 pm	
	24/3/17		Nothing to Report	
	25/3/17		do	
	26/3/17		109th Brigade Signals investigated Scheme of communication with Battalions, and a Central Brigade Station at ROUVELINGHEM [illegible]	ROUVELINGHEM

Army Form C. 2118.

WAR DIARY
or
INTELLIGENCE SUMMARY 36th Div Signal Coy R.E.

(Erase heading not required.)

Place	Date	Hour	Summary of Events and Information	Remarks and references to Appendices
In the Field	27/3/17		Nothing to report	
	28/3/17		do	
	29/3/17		Signalling competition arranged by 109th Brigade was had to be postponed owing to bad weather.	
	30/3/17		Circuits of 10 S.W. cable extended to forward areas	
	31/3/17		do	

MMaurer Lieut R.E.
for O.C. 36th Div Sig Coy R.E.

Army Form C. 2118.

Vol 19
364th Div. Signal Coy. R.E.

WAR DIARY
or
INTELLIGENCE SUMMARY
(Erase heading not required.)

Place	Date	Hour	Summary of Events and Information	Remarks and references to Appendices
In the Field	1.4.17		2nd Lieut S.L. Smith & R. Zouw two joined for duty with Signals	
			108th Inf Brigade	
	2.4.17		Lieut T.G. Johnston & R. Zouw two joined for duty	
	3.4.17		Nothing to report	
	4.4.17		No. 4 Section commenced march from Second Army training area	
			to Brouwine billeting for night at Argues	
	5.4.17		No. 3 Section carried out Buzzer practice with battn. signal sections	
	6.4.17		No. 4 Section continued march to Brouwine where Section arrived	
			for two nights previous to being moved from No. 2 Section area up	
			No. 3 Section Battalions moved to BERTHEN training area	
			Communication established with 121st and 136th Inf Bdes	
			by telephone	
	7.4.17		Nothing to report	
	8.4.17		No. 4 Section (Argues Bde.) took over from & No. 2 Section (109th Bde.) in	
			SPANBROEKE Sector	
	9.4.17		No. 3 Sigw. Bde. Hqrs. moved to BERTHEN. Communication	
			established with 120 & 136 R.I.R. by telephone	

Army Form C. 2118.

WAR DIARY
or
INTELLIGENCE SUMMARY. 36th Div Signal Coy RE

(Erase heading not required.)

Place	Date	Hour	Summary of Events and Information	Remarks and references to Appendices
In the Field	10.4.17		No. 3 Section 108th M.G. Coy and 108th T.M.B. moved to DIEBROUCK from Wolvers. Communication established by orderly	
"	11.4.17		2nd Lieut T. Dodd (Durham R.I.) took over command of No 1 Section vice Lieut R.T. Dudley RE transferred to "E" Corps Signal School as Commandant	
"	12.4.17		No 3 Section picked up communication between 9th R. Irish and Ulster Rifles joined through on semi-permanent line from MT. DES CATS to BERTHEN giving telephonic communication with two Battalions named	
"	13.4.17		Nothing to Report	
"	14.4.17		No. 3 Section took part in Field Day with Battalions. Breakers attacked group through. Very successful work done by contact aircraft camera	
"	15.4.17		No. 2 Section C107th Bde left for Second Army Training Area (BOUKELINGHEM) Lieut T.G. Johnston 9th R. Irish Fus. rejoined this unit	
"	16.4.17		Nothing to report. No 3 Section (108th Bde)	
"	17.4.17		Carried out communications for Bde Brigade attack. Successful Field Day	

WAR DIARY

36th Div Signal Coy RE   Army Form C. 2118.

INTELLIGENCE SUMMARY.
(Erase heading not required.)

Place	Date	Hour	Summary of Events and Information	Remarks and references to Appendices
In the Field	18.4.17		2nd Lieut G H Butter and reported No 4 Section (109th) Inf Bde) from Second Army Signal School.	
"	19.4.17		No 3 Section Bde Hqrs moved to DRANOUTRE	
"	20.4.17		Nothing to report	
"	21.4.17		Brigade Signalling Competition held by No 3 Section	
"	22.4.17		Nothing to report	
"	23.4.17		No 3 Section (108th Inf Bde) First day of three days training of scheme for communication on the attack, good results obtained from power Buzzers and Amplifiers, work satisfactory	
"	24.4.17		Second day of Bde signal scheme 110th R.E. & Signal Coy assisted in signalled Practice	
"	25.4.17		Third day of above signalled of 108th and 13th R and R Bde practiced	
"	26.4.17		Nothing to Report	
"	27.4.17		do	
"	28.4.17		do	
"	29.4.17		do	

No 2 Section (107 Inf Bde) returning from Second Army Training Area ARQUES. Officer opened of ARQUES 2.15PM

[Signature] Lieut. RE for OC 36th Div Sig Coy RE

WAR DIARY
or
INTELLIGENCE SUMMARY.
(Erase heading not required.)

Army Form C. 2118.

Place	Date	Hour	Summary of Events and Information	Remarks and references to Appendices
	1/5/17 – 23/5/17		Company engaged in preparing Buried Cable System in forward area	
	24/5/17	9 p.m.	108 Infantry Bde Sig. Office HQ moved to HQs relieving 109 Infantry Bde Signal Office at 9 p.m.	
	25/5/17		Front Sig. Office from Spanbroekmolen to White Camp Kemmel. Electric route to HQs not constructed.	
			108 Infantry Bde Sig HQ moved to J.17.b.8. Sig. Office opened to Bn. Communication established between Brigade HQ and Battalion, Artillery Group Divisions and Lateral Brigades	
	27/5/17		Severe shelling of Check Areas. Route liable to be damaged – Route cut by shell fire but quickly mended.	
	28/5/17		Divisional HQ moved to J.17.a.8 displacing 108 Inf Bde who moved to J.17.b.4 Signal Office at 3 p.m. At night shelling to front. On the HQ Bde & coy. Repairs turned out quickly.	
	29/5/17		Enemy Artillery in regard to Ligny ca Cable Routes in 108 Bde area but repairs were successfully effected	
	30/5/17 – 31/5/17		Shelling continued during some hours to our T.S. Brigade Communications to Infantry purposes re R.E. and Gas horseshoe established	

for O.C. 38 Divl Sig Co

11/6/17

Army Form C. 2118.

WAR DIARY
INTELLIGENCE SUMMARY.
(Erase heading not required.)

36th Div. Signal Coy

Vol 2

Place	Date	Hour	Summary of Events and Information	Remarks and references to Appendices
	1/6/17		Company engaged in marking routes on Buried Cable system	
	2/6/17		Company preparing Amplifier Earths. Cable trench dug from Front line trenches into cottage in "No Man's Land" and partly drained.	
	3/6/17		Night working party cleared cottage of water.	
In the field	4/6/17		Amplifier Earths dug in. Special Communication for raid by 13th R.I. Rifles completed and worked satisfactorily under trying conditions.	
	5/6/17		Test Board fitted in cottage in "No Man's Land". Communication for raid by 9th R. Ir. Fusiliers established from point of exit in Front line to covering batteries, remaining good throughout. Repairs were effected by 6.0 am following day.	
	6/6/17		Amplifier Earths and Communication generally, for Offensive completed Attack on WYTSCHAETE - MESSINES Ridge. At Zero hour communication to Infantry Brigades consists of two buried circuits each. Cable trench dug from HQ. to Scott Farm, distance 1200 yards. Joints made and Test Boards fitted 8.0 p.m. Communication from 108th Infantry	
	7/6/17		Brigade HQ. to all Battalions operating under them established on Air Line	

Army Form C. 2118.

WAR DIARY
or
INTELLIGENCE SUMMARY.
(Erase heading not required.)

Instructions regarding War Diaries and Intelligence Summaries are contained in F. S. Regs., Part II. and the Staff Manual respectively. Title pages will be prepared in manuscript.

Place	Date	Hour	Summary of Events and Information	Remarks and references to Appendices
In the Field	8/6/17		Communication between Brigades and Battalions supplemented by establishment of Power Buzzers and Amplifier Stations. Visual Signalling between Divisional Visual Station on Kemmel Hill and Forward Stations working satisfactorily relieving pressure on Telephone Circuits. Pigeons ready for use but not actually required. Airlines to Battalions frequently cut but quickly repaired.	
	9/6/17		Division Hq. on relief by 11th Division moved to St Jans Cappel. Signal Office opening 3.0 p.m.	
	19/6/17		Divisional Visual Station re-established at Kemmel Tower.	
	20/6/17		Divisional H.Q. moved to Pradelles relieving 11th Division. Signal Office opening 10.0 a.m.	
	30/6/17		On Relief by 19th Division, Division Hq. moved to Morris Area. Signal Office opening 10.0 a.m.	

for O.C. 36th Div. Sig Co. R.E.
Capt. R.E.

Vol 22

Army Form C. 2118.

WAR DIARY
or
INTELLIGENCE SUMMARY. 36 Signal Coy, RE
(Erase heading not required.)

Instructions regarding War Diaries and Intelligence Summaries are contained in F. S. Regs., Part II. and the Staff Manual respectively. Title pages will be prepared in manuscript.

Place	Date	Hour	Summary of Events and Information	Remarks and references to Appendices
In the Field	July 1 to July 31, 1917		During the month of July the Signal Company was located in the Training Area. Brigade Schemes in conjunction with the Infantry were carried out successfully. Communication whilst in the WIZERNES area was maintained by Wireless and Visual.	

8/8/17

For O.C. 36th Div. Sig. Coy R.E

36th Divl. Signal Coy RE.
Army Form C. 2118.

WA 23

WAR DIARY
INTELLIGENCE SUMMARY
(Erase heading not required.)

Place	Date	Hour	Summary of Events and Information	Remarks and references to Appendices
In the Field	1/8/17		Company HQ in Poperinghe.	
			Nos. 2 & 4 Sections in Watou area	
			No. 3 Section in VLAMERTINGHE	
	2/8/17	4:20am	No. 2 Section moved from WATOU area to WIELTJE and relieved the Sections of 164, 165 and 166 Bdes in the line. In addition to existing lines, ran lateral pair of D1 cable from CALL RESERVE to UHLAN FARM. Battalions at PLUM FARM and C29c9.6 in communication to Brigade by runner only.	
	3/8/17		No. 2 Section ran two pairs cable from Bde HQ to UHLAN FARM and lateral pair from CALL RES. to 15th R.I.R. (C23c9.6).	
			No. 3 Section moved to BRANDHOEK AREA.	
			No. 4 Section moved to camp on YPRES – POPERINGHE RD.	
	4/8/17		Divisional Signal Office closed down at POPERINGHE. 11 onwards opened	

Army Form C. 2118.

WAR DIARY
or
INTELLIGENCE SUMMARY.
(Erase heading not required.)

Instructions regarding War Diaries and Intelligence Summaries are contained in F.S. Regs., Part II. and the Staff Manual respectively. Title pages will be prepared in manuscript.

Place	Date	Hour	Summary of Events and Information	Remarks and references to Appendices
In the field	4/6/17	(Contd)	Office at Morbecq Camp same hour.	
			No. 2 Bde Section repaired all Battalion lines which had been cut by shell fire.	
			Company forward Party.	
			Poled cable route from SH - E15 dugout cut in eleven places by shellfire, and repaired. Their armoured cable in GARDEN ST., cut twice by shell present repaired.	
	5/6/17		107th Bde intercom line disconnected at 8.20 pm.	
			No 2 Bde Section arranged visual signalling with Bde on left by Lucas lamp. Shetel, shelling was very heavy all day. Lines were cut and repaired in many places. Three plug and socket boards were fitted in No. 9 dugout armoured cables run into 107th Bde	
			WIELTJE. 24 pr. armoured cable and wired on to board. Lead cable route wired on to board in 107 Bde signal Office.	

WAR DIARY

Army Form C. 2118.

INTELLIGENCE SUMMARY
(Erase heading not required.)

Place	Date	Hour	Summary of Events and Information	Remarks and references to Appendices
In the Field	6/8/17		10 pm Bde vibrator line found disconnected (wrongly bridged in AD dug out) was put through. Repaires held cable route which had been cut in five places by shellfire. No. 2 Bde Section repaired lines to Life Battn. and Bde at MILLCOT also lines from UHLAN FARM to PLUM FARM and from UHLAN FARM to BDE. Linesmen were almost constantly out on breaks caused by hostile shellfire.	
	7/8/17	7:15 pm	Somewhat fatty up 16-line Exchange in No 9 dugout WIELTJE Company, fitted it to Plug & socket board. 7:15 pm wire from CANAL BANK to DIV. H.Q. disconnected owing to charges. This was put through again in half an hour. 4 pr. lead cable between E and AD dugouts (which had been cut for some weeks) was repaired. No 2 Section doubled lateral line from UHLAN FARM to	

WAR DIARY
INTELLIGENCE SUMMARY.
(Erase heading not required.)

Army Form C. 2118.

Place	Date	Hour	Summary of Events and Information	Remarks and references to Appendices
In the Field	7/8/17 (contd)		CALL RES. At about 10pm "SOS" signals came through from all battalions and heavy bombardment commenced on both sides. Both lines to Right Batn. and one to left Batn., cut but communication was carried on by means of lateral lines. Lines were repaired after firing had died down. Lines were relieved by No. 3 Bde section on right U/S lines were handed over all through and relief completed 4.30am.	
	8/8/17		Forward Sect. Company "put" through 188th Bde to DIV. H.Q. by direct insulator line, also 153 Bde RFA to DIV. H.Q. Brought armoured house into use between S and SC dugouts. Put Canal Bank Stn through to 178 Bde RFA (speaking line) via AD-E-F-O dugouts. Issued out 7/p Contact bad cable between SH and AD dugouts on 108 Bde to DIV. H.Q. vibrator line between LG dugout	

Army Form C. 2118.

WAR DIARY
INTELLIGENCE SUMMARY
(Erase heading not required.)

Place	Date	Hour	Summary of Events and Information	Remarks and references to Appendices
In the field	8/8/17 (Cont)		and CANAL BANK station. Contact on 173 Bde R.F.A. and 108 Infantry Bde lines.	
	9/8/17		Company forward party tested out 9 pr lines between E and AD dugouts. Several ordinary faults cleared.	
	10/8/17		Company forward party ran lines in WIELTJE TUNNEL to provide for incoming units. Several trunk lines put through AD - 1B - EL dugouts	

Army Form C. 2118.

WAR DIARY
INTELLIGENCE SUMMARY.
(Erase heading not required.)

Instructions regarding War Diaries and Intelligence Summaries are contained in F. S. Regs., Part II. and the Staff Manual respectively. Title pages will be prepared in manuscript.

Place	Date	Hour	Summary of Events and Information	Remarks and references to Appendices
Enfield				
	11/9/17		Company Fwd Party commenced 4 ft route WIELTJE to MILLCOTTS. Lines taped out between E & W and WAP dugouts.	
			No. 2 Bde section relieved No. 4 Bde section in line, HQ. WIELTJE DUGOUTS.	
	12/9/17		Company Fwd. Party continued their route from WIELTJE to MILLCOTTS	

Army Form C. 2118.

WAR DIARY
or
INTELLIGENCE SUMMARY.
(Erase heading not required.)

Instructions regarding War Diaries and Intelligence Summaries are contained in F. S. Regs., Part II. and the Staff Manual respectively. Title pages will be prepared in manuscript.

Place	Date	Hour	Summary of Events and Information	Remarks and references to Appendices
In the field	17/6/17 (contd)		Cable dump established at C.P. Sqn (Canal Bank)	
	13/9/17	5 am	No. 2 Adv. Section relief completed. Found five pairs German buried lines in CALL RES. Patrol sent out to POMMERN CASTLE at night but failed to get signals through on these pairs. Reinforcements to forward party reported at Canal Bank. Pairs put through on new buried from Lc — S dugouts. These route finished.	
	14/9/17		No. 2 Section ran lines to WIELTJE FARM for Support Bttn. and strengthened all existing lines. Were relieved in line by No. 3 Y4 Sections. Staff and battalions returning to VLAMERTINGHE AREA.	

A6945 Wt. W11422/M1160 350,000 12/16 D. D. & L. Forms/C./2118/14.

Army Form C. 2118.

WAR DIARY
INTELLIGENCE SUMMARY.
(Erase heading not required.)

Instructions regarding War Diaries and Intelligence Summaries are contained in F.S. Regs., Part II. and the Staff Manual respectively. Title pages will be prepared in manuscript.

Place	Date	Hour	Summary of Events and Information	Remarks and references to Appendices
In the Field	14/8/17 (Contd)		Coy. Forward Party leaving out more para W-P dugouts. Carrying and reconnoitring party went up to BANK FARM in the evening	
	15/8/17		No. 2 B.C. Section remained at MIL COT with stores. Ran line to WARWICK FARM for 9th R. Ir. Rifles. Plugged line through at #108 Bde S.H. to WIELTJE FARM for 8th R. I. Rifles. Arranged line via "F" dugout and "E12" dugout to VINERY for 10th and 15th R. Ir. Rifles. Company Fwd: Party laid out line from WIELTJE to BANK F.M. Cables runners relay route at night.	
	16/8/17	4.45am	ZERO.	
		5am	No. 2 Bde section repaired line to 8th R. Ir. Rifles. Remainder of their line held all day. They were ordered to take over line night of 16/17. Ran line to UHLAN FARM and laid out from	

Army Form C. 2118.

WAR DIARY
INTELLIGENCE SUMMARY.
(Erase heading not required.)

Instructions regarding War Diaries and Intelligence Summaries are contained in F. S. Regs., Part II. and the Staff Manual respectively. Title pages will be prepared in manuscript.

Place	Date	Hour	Summary of Events and Information	Remarks and references to Appendices
In the field	16/9/17		CALL FARM 6 AVV	
	17/9/17			
	18/9/17	3 pm	Relieved by 61st. Div'l. Signal Coy and moved to WINNEZEELE. Office closed at MERSEY CAMP 3 pm. and opened WINNEZEELE at same hour.	
	19/9/17			

Army Form C. 2118.

WAR DIARY
INTELLIGENCE SUMMARY.
(Erase heading not required.)

Instructions regarding War Diaries and Intelligence Summaries are contained in F. S. Regs., Part II, and the Staff Manual respectively. Title pages will be prepared in manuscript.

Place	Date	Hour	Summary of Events and Information	Remarks and references to Appendices
In the field	20/9/17			
	21/9/17			
	22/9/17			
	23/9/17	12 noon	Signal Office closed at WINNEZEELE and Company moved by train, entraining at ESQUELBECQ, to Third Army area.	
	24/9/17	6.30am	Upon relieving 59th Divn Signal Office opened at BARASTRE.	
	25/9/17			
	26/9/17		NCO's and men sent to 9th Divn HQ to become acquainted with the system of communication.	

Army Form C. 2118.

WAR DIARY
INTELLIGENCE SUMMARY.
(Erase heading not required.)

Instructions regarding War Diaries and Intelligence Summaries are contained in F. S. Regs., Part II. and the Staff Manual respectively. Title pages will be prepared in manuscript.

Place	Date	Hour	Summary of Events and Information	Remarks and references to Appendices
In the field	27/8/17			
	28/8/17			
	29/8/17			
	30/8/17			
	31/8/17	10am	Relieved 9th Divl. Signal Coy. (in the line) Signal Office closed at BARASTRE and opened YPRES same hour.	

J. S. Shaw Lt. R.E. for O.C. 36th Divl Signal Coy R.E.

SECRET

Army Form C. 2118.

WAR DIARY
or
INTELLIGENCE SUMMARY.
(Erase heading not required.)

Instructions regarding War Diaries and Intelligence Summaries are contained in F.S. Regs., Part II. and the Staff Manual respectively. Title pages will be prepared in manuscript.

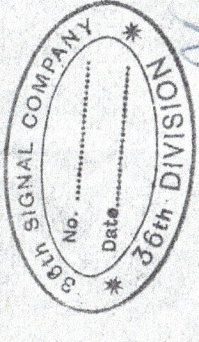

36th SIGNAL COMPANY / 36th DIVISION

WW 24

Place	Date	Hour	Summary of Events and Information	Remarks and references to Appendices
In the Field	1/9/17	----	Completed wiring off office at TTR. Ran wire to new H.Q. 131 Field Coy. R.E.	
do	2/9/17	----	Ran 2 lines RBR to FD for new Bn. H.Q. at COSY DUMP. Tested out 4 pairs on bury TRESCAULT AVE. to Ll and ran 2 pairs to Bl to connect up. 109Bde ran line from Rt. Battn. to Rt. Coy. which ran direct replaced by new line along trench.	
do	3/9/17	----	107th Bde. Reeled up RBR 15. Took over new Bn front and Bn H.Q. at B 2 and arranged lines.	
do	4/9/17	----	Put through new lines for B 2 at FD. Ran pairs Bl - B 2 for lateral. picked up lines in bury for Coy. lines Ll - BB. Arranged Coy. laterals. 1 Drum of old cable salvaged.	
do	6/9/17	----	Put through RBR 14 on bury to L. 1. 109th Bde A.S.Capt's office connected by Phone to Div. Res. Bn. in BERTINCOURT.	
do	6/9/17	----	Work done on lines B2 - Bl and TTG - B 2.	
do	7/9/17	----	Tested pairs of KJ bury. Picked up cable in METZ. 109th Bde. Lines laid from Left Bn. to L. Section M.G.Coy.	
do	8/9/17	----	Signal Lamps placed in position for Observation Balloon. Forward lines labelled Repaired and maintained lines to B 1	
do	9/9/17	----	Terminal Strips erected leading to HAVRINCOURT WOOD and general straightening of lines, more especially those running across roads etc. which had been left in a deplorable state, unlabelled, straggling across roads etc.	
do	10/9/17	----	Took up cable to L 1. Ran out cable for party at night. Commenced burying line Ll - Ll B. Pigeon service resumed 109th Bde. Bde O.P. connected to M.G. Coy. line.	
do	11/9/17	----	Continued with buried line at night. 109th Bde. About this time the first of a series of cases of cable being deliberately cut out of working lines occurred; it continued for 3 days, usually pieces of 600 yds being cut out. Men were posted & D.S. Forms 6/32 Lts look out but failed to discover the culprits.	

Army Form C. 2118.

WAR DIARY
or
INTELLIGENCE SUMMARY

(Erase heading not required.)

Instructions regarding War Diaries and Intelligence Summaries are contained in F. S. Regs., Part II. and the Staff Manual respectively. Title Pages will be prepared in manuscript.

Place	Date	Hour	Summary of Events and Information	Remarks and references to Appendices
In the field	12/9/17		Repaired line L1 RBR. Worked on buried line.	
do	13/9/17		Worked on buries	
do	14/9/17		do	
do	15/9/17		Strengthened routes TTR - RBR and TTR-TTC. Worked on bury at night. 109th Bde. O.P. connected by Phone to both Battns. in line.	
do	16/9/17		Visual communication arranged between Bde. O.P. and Coys. in line. Took up Cable from TRESCAULT Dump. Enemy Artillery active; between 200 and 300 shells being fired into cemetery at J 33 a.	
do	17/9/17		Advanced Field Coy. connected by Phone to Rt. Battn.	
do	18/9/17		Dug in 42 lateral pairs to L1. Commenced to run leads to terminal boards at L1. Worked on buried lines at night.	
do	19/9/17		Continued working on bury L 1 B. New 7 pr. route brought into TTK office.	
do	20/9/17		159th Field Coy. R.E. connected to TTK by ringing Phone. Old Cable reeled in. Continued work on bury L1 B	
do	21/9/17		Battery position at Q.7.a.1.4 was deliberately shelled by enemy 10.5 cm. and 15 cm. Hos. from 11 a.m. to 7.30 p.m. Line to Brigade was mended 9 times in 4 hours	
do	22/9/17		Continued work on bury L1 B. Put B2 - BB line through on L1-B2 bury. Worked on bury at night.	

Army Form C. 2118.

WAR DIARY
or
INTELLIGENCE SUMMARY
(Erase heading not required.)

Instructions regarding War Diaries and Intelligence Summaries are contained in F.S. Regs., Part II and the Staff Manual respectively. Title Pages will be prepared in manuscript.

Place	Date	Hour	Summary of Events and Information	Remarks and references to Appendices
In the Field	23/9/17		Test out lines on KJ bury for RFA. Put 4 prs. through K 132 and 3 prs. K-L1	
do	24/9/17		Worked on buried lines	
do	25/9/17		Worked on buried lines	
do	26/9/17		Worked on buried lines. Collected cable, sorted and repaired same. Adv. Field Coys now connected to Bde. Test Point.	
do	27/9/17		Started working on new 7 pr. route. Position calls brought into force. Ran lines to METZ pole to join up with line to Bde. on left. Worked on bury at night.	
do	28/9/17		Worked on buried lines	
do	29/9/17		Wagon Lines at BUS connected to BUS EXCHANGE. Worked on buried lines at night. Duplicate lines laid from 109th Bde. Signal Office to emergency Dugout.	
do	30/9/17		109th laid line to Left Sec. M.G.Coy.	

Capt. RE
for O.C. 36th Divl Sig Coy, RE

1/10/17

SECRET

Army Form C. 2118.

36D Signal
JK 25

WAR DIARY
or
INTELLIGENCE SUMMARY
(Erase heading not required.)

Instructions regarding War Diaries and Intelligence Summaries are contained in F. S. Regs., Part II. and the Staff Manual respectively. Title Pages will be prepared in manuscript.

Place	Date	Hour	Summary of Events and Information	Remarks and references to Appendices
In the Field	1/10/17		Picking up and clearing old line in HAVRINCOURT WOOD.	
"	2/10/17		do	
"	3/10/17		Labelling and work on buried lines.	
"	4/10/17		Working on lines.	
"	5/10/17		Worked on buried lines. Put Right Group through on old M.G. Coy. line and bury.	
"	6/10/17		Laid new line to Right Battn. from L dugout	
"	7/10/17		Staking routes and work on buried lines	
"	8/10/17		Working on lines in St HUBERT'S AVENUE and CAMPBELL WYND	
"	9/10/17		Reeling up HW and HE route. Cleared fault on P53 and P 54. Worked on bury at night but had to stop on account of Gas Shells	
"	10/10/17		Cable party moved to new camp at Q.14. Central. Worked on bury at night	
"	11/10/17		173rd Bde. R.F.A. staked routes	
"	12/10/17		Buried 2 spares of P.80 and P81. Work on bury stopped by rain	
"	13/10/17		Overhauled line to P78. Worked on bury at night and repaired P80 and P81	
"	14/10/17		do	
"	15/10/17		Completed new staked route between SOMERSET Spur and L. Battn. H.Q. worked on bury at night. Line running to D173 Batty. 173rd Bde. R.F.A. is diverted on to staked route running from SLAG HEAP along bank of Canal.	

SECRET

Army Form C. 2118.

WAR DIARY
or
INTELLIGENCE SUMMARY
(Erase heading not required.)

Instructions regarding War Diaries and Intelligence Summaries are contained in F. S. Regs., Part II. and the Staff Manual respectively. Title Pages will be prepared in manuscript.

Place	Date	Hour	Summary of Events and Information	Remarks and references to Appendices
In the Fld	16/10/17		Worked on buried lines.	
"	17/10/17		Worked on lines in St. HUBERT'S AVENUE. Putting in new staked route.	
"	19/10/17		Worked on new staked routes in ST. HUBERT'S AVE. Worked on bury at night	
"	19/10/17		do	
"	20/10/17		do	
"	21/10/17		Put lines through on bury from M.G. Coy. to Adv. H.Q. to O.P. near BILHEM Farm (107th Bde.)	
"	22/10/17		107th Bde. Commenced bury from Left Battn. to Companies in line. Labelling lines and working in ST.HUBERT'S AVE.	
"	23/10/17		Worked on bury at night. Wired P. & S. boards in "C" Dugout	
"	24/10/17		do	
"	25/10/17		Laid new staked route between HW and MILL FARM and between P67 and HENLEY AVE. Worked on buried lines at night.	
"	26/10/17		Route erected at BERTINCOURT between 109th Inf. Bde. H.Q. and 173rd Arty. Bde. H.Q. Staked route from P67 to HENLEY AVE completed Worked on N - hW route.	
"	27/10/17		Patrolling, labelling and fixing lines on staked routes. Worked in ST.HUBERT'S AVE. and staked route between HW and MILL FM. Line run out to Lone Gun of "C" Batty. 173rd. Bde. R.F.A. and One from D 173 to "C" 173rd Bde.	

SECRET

Army Form C. 2118.

WAR DIARY
or
INTELLIGENCE SUMMARY
(Erase heading not required.)

Instructions regarding War Diaries and Intelligence Summaries are contained in F. S. Regs., Part II. and the Staff Manual respectively. Title Pages will be prepared in manuscript.

Place	Date	Hour	Summary of Events and Information	Remarks and references to Appendices
In the Fd.	28/10/17		Worked on buried lines at night	
	29/10/17		Worked on buried lines at night. Staked route between HW and MILL FM. Completed labelling lines at 108th Bde. and reeling in old wire.	
	30/10/17		Tightening up lines in HUBERT ROAD. Labeeling lines. Picking up old wire. Worked on lines at BERTINCOURT.	
	31/10/17		Labelling lines and petrolling staked routes. Work at BERTINCOURT continued.	

1.11.17.

[signature] Capt. R.E.,
for O.C. 36th Div. Signal Coy. R.E.

SECRET

Army Form C. 2118.

36th Signal Coy. R.E
Vol 26

WAR DIARY
or
INTELLIGENCE SUMMARY.
(Erase heading not required.)

Instructions regarding War Diaries and Intelligence Summaries are contained in F. S. Regs., Part II. and the Staff Manual respectively. Title pages will be prepared in manuscript.

Place	Date Nov/8	Hour	Summary of Events and Information	Remarks and references to Appendices
In the Field	1	-----	R.A. Offices burnt down	
	5	-----	Capt. H.A.M. Napier, A.& S.H. joined for duty	
	6	-----	Capt. W.J. Howe went to Hospital	
	7	-----	Preparations for attack being made. 51st Div Signals took over Right Bde. Sector for work 62 " " " Centre " " " " 36th " " concentrate on left Bde. " " " A system of suspended 7 pr lead covered and staked 7 pr brass sheathed cable laid out with Advanced Headquarters at HERMIES	
		20	153 T92 R.F.A. Operations commence. Communications stood well. Established Visual Station at H.S near HERMIES at zero hour, communication kept up all day excepting line to F.O.O. which was cut several times, light was very bad for Visual Work but some useful information was received by Lucas Lamp from F.O.O. In the afternoon lines were laid out from forward H.Q. to proposed forward battery positions also got in touch with Division through H.S's and Artillery Brigade H.Q. (forward) on our right. At 8 p.m. received information that 153rd Brigade R.F.A. would come into action by 7 a.m. next morning on the West side of Canal Du Nord near DEMICOURT so withdrew Cable Cart and party back to METZ and advanced with 153rd Brigade that night, evacuating Exchange at METZ	
	21	-----	Two Cable detachments laid two pairs from Spoil Heap in K30 Central to GRAINCOURT for 107th Brigade and 93rd R.F.A. Bde. 163 T92 RFAH.Q. established at K.7.d.00.20 and Batteries came into action about 400 yards East of this point to be ready for action by 10 a.m. All communications established by this hour. mending lines and laying same all day. also Visual communication established with all batteries and Brigades (Artillery) on our right. Telephone communication also established with latter.	

(A7283) Wt.W807/1672 550.000 4/17 Sch 52a Forms/C/2118/4

Army Form C. 2118.

WAR DIARY
or
INTELLIGENCE SUMMARY.
(Erase heading not required.)

Instructions regarding War Diaries and Intelligence Summaries are contained in F.S. Regs., Part II, and the Staff Manual respectively. Title pages will be prepared in manuscript.

Place	Date Nov	Hour	Summary of Events and Information	Remarks and references to Appendices
In the Field	22	---	Maintenance and improvement of lines. Conditions getting worse. Laying out line to F.O.O. and Brigade O.P., Visual established with same.	
	23	---	Mending lines and got direct line to 93rd Bde. R.F.A. (Bde on our right)	Copy of til to time. 153
	27	---	Relieved by 2nd Division and moved to LITTLE WOOD near YPRES. All Bde. R.F.A. H.Q. moved to broken bridge 100 yards south of LOCK 7. communication established by 5 p.m. also direct line to 41st Bde. R.F.A. laid.	
	28	---	2/Lt. G.M. Cooper joined for Duty.	
	29	---	Transport marched from LITTLE WOOD to FOSSEUX about 28 miles, leaving LITTLE WOOD 3 a.m. and getting into FOSSEUX at 1 p.m. personnel marched to BAPAUME to entrain, detrained at BEAUMETZ and marched to FOSSEUX.	
	30	Enemy	Left FOSSEUX 4.15 p.m. and marched back to ACHIET LE PETIT. Only Communication counter attacked many lines cut by shell-fire but communications kept up all day excepting our direct line to 2nd Division, which was cut early in morning by shell-fire.	
			Casualties during month. Officers NIL, O.R. Killed One, Missing NIL WOUNDED Three.	

A. Mahon
Capt. A. & S.H.
for O.C. 36th Divl. Sig. Coy., R.E.

Army Form C. 2118.

36th Signal Cy. RE

WAR DIARY
INTELLIGENCE SUMMARY
(Erase heading not required.)

Instructions regarding War Diaries and Intelligence Summaries are contained in F.S. Regs., Part II. and the Staff Manual respectively. Title Pages will be prepared in manuscript.

Place	Date	Hour	Summary of Events and Information	Remarks and references to Appendices
In the Field	1/12/17		Moved from ACHIET-LE-PETIT to YTRES. Artillery laid out new lines to Lock No. 7 (HERMIES) to obtain communication with Div.	
"	2/12/17		"A" Battery, 153rd Bde., R.F.A., shelled heavily, lines being cut twice in afternoon.	
"	3/12/17		New line laid to Infantry Brigade Headquarters at Lock 7, by 153rd Bde. R.F.A. Lateral lines to 173rd Bde. cut twice during day by enemy shell fire.	
"	4/12/17		Moved from YTRES to SOREL	
"	5/12/17		108th Bde. Section moved to Dugout in HINDENBURG Support Line relieving 182nd Bde. Section. 153rd Bde. R.F.A. moved to new Headquarters at HERMIES. Communication established with New Battery Positions. 108th Bde. Section relieved 187th Inf. Bde. Section. 107th Inf. Bde. in HETZ	
"	6/12/17		153rd Bde. H.Q. at Broken Bridge near Lock 7 evacuated.	
"	7/12/17		109th Inf. Bde. Sig. Section relieved 107th Inf. Bde. Section.	
"	8/12/17		Nothing to report	
"	9/12/17		Lines to Batteries repaired by 153rd Bde. R.F.A., having been broken by traffic	
"	10/12/17		Lines laid to Battns. by 108th Bde. Section.	
"	11/12/17		Nothing to report	
"	12/12/17		153rd Bde. R.F.A. moved to new H.Q. Spare cable picked up.	
"	13/12/17		Nothing to report	
"	14/12/17		Lines laid and exchanges wired by 153rd Bde., R.F.A.	
"	15/12/17		108th Inf. Bde. Section moved from FINS to ROCQUIGNY. Communication with Division established through 5th Corps.	

Army Form C. 2118.

WAR DIARY
or
INTELLIGENCE SUMMARY
(Erase heading not required.)

Instructions regarding War Diaries and Intelligence Summaries are contained in F.S. Regs., Part II. and the Staff Manual respectively. Title Pages will be prepared in manuscript.

Place	Date	Hour	Summary of Events and Information	Remarks and references to Appendices
In the Field	16/12/17		106th Inf. Bde. Section entrained at ETRICOURT for MONDICOURT thence to HALLOY. 107th Bde. Section stated at MANANCOURT 108th Inf. Bde. Section relieved by 106th Inf. Bde. Section.	
"	17/12/17		108th Inf. Bde. Section moved to ETRICOURT. 107th Inf. Bde. Section entrained at ETRICOURT and detrained at MONDICOURT and marched to IVERGNY	
"	18/12/17		Div. moved from SOREL to LUCHEUX	
"	19/12/17		do	
"	20/12/17		do	
"	21/12/17		do	
"	22/12/17		Lines laid out to Brigades	
"	23/12/17		Nothing to report	
"	24/12/17		do	
"	25/12/17		do	
"	26/12/17		do	
"	27/12/17		Div. moved from LUCHEUX area to CORBIE area	
"	28/12/17		do	
"	29/12/17		do	
"	30/12/17		Lines laid out and maintained to Brigades.	
"	31.12.17		Communication established with all units	

SECRET

Army Form C. 2118.

36D 3 Signal
Vol 28

WAR DIARY
~~INTELLIGENCE SUMMARY~~
(Erase heading not required.)

36th DIV. SIG. COY. R.E.

Instructions regarding War Diaries and Intelligence Summaries are contained in F. S. Regs., Part II. and the Staff Manual respectively. Title Pages will be prepared in manuscript.

Place	Date	Hour	Summary of Events and Information	Remarks and references to Appendices
In the Field	1/1/18	---	Nothing to report	
"	2/1/18	---	do	
"	3/1/18	---	do	
"	4/1/18	---	do	
"	5/1/18	---	do	
"	6/1/18	---	do	
"	7/1/18	---	Moved from CORBIE to HARBONNIERES. Office closed CORBIE 10 a.m. and opened same hour at HARBONNIERES.	
"	8/1/18	---	Nothing to report	
"	9/1/18	---	do	
"	10/1/18	---	do	
"	11/1/18	---	do	
"	12/1/18	---	Moved from HARBONNIERES to NESLE. Office closed HARBONNIERES E 3 p.m. opened NESLE 12 noon.	
"	13/1/18	---	do	
"	14/1/18	---	Moved from NESLE to OLLEZEY. Office closed NESLE 10 a.m. and opened OLLEZEY.	
"	15/1/18	---	Work on communications commenced in new area taken over from the French. Visual stations tested.	

Army Form C. 2118.

Instructions regarding War Diaries and Intelligence Summaries are contained in F.S. Regs, Part II. and the Staff Manual respectively. Title Pages will be prepared in manuscript.

WAR DIARY
or
INTELLIGENCE SUMMARY
(Erase heading not required.)

38th DIV SIG. COY. R.E.

Place	Date	Hour	Summary of Events and Information	Remarks and references to Appendices
In the Field	16/1/18		Forward Exchange established at GRAND SERAUCOURT. Lines laid out, repaired and patrolled. Telephone exchange at ST MARTIN taken over from French.	
"	17/1/18		Patrolling and repairing lines and completing left Group Communications	
"	18/1/18		No. 3 Section moved from ESTOUILLY to DURY.	
"	19/1/18		Improvements made to ST MARIE Exchange. Lines poled. Lines repaired by No. 2 Section. New cable laid by No. 4 Section to Left Battn. of 109th Inf. Brigade	
"	20/1/18		New lines laid by No. 4 Section to Right Battalion, 109th Inf. Bde. and to Visual Receiving Station. New line laid to Left Battalion 107th Inf Bde. by No. 2 Section.	
"	21/1/18		No. 2 section continued work on new O.P. and repaired line to Support Battalion of 107th Inf. Bde. Lines overhauled	
"	22/1/18		Power Buzzers and Amplifier installed in 109th Bde. area	
"	23/1/18		Patrolling and repairing lines and completing communications	
"	24/1/18		do	
"	25/1/18		do	
"	26/1/18		New lines laid out by Nos. 2 and 4 Sections.	
"	27/1/18		Communication between Power Buzzers and Amplifier established by No. 4 Section	
"	28/1/18		Lines repaired and patrolled	
"	29/1/18		Lines cleared up in trenches	

Army Form C. 2118.

WAR DIARY
or
INTELLIGENCE SUMMARY

36th DIV. SIG. COY. R.E. *(Erase heading not required.)*

Instructions regarding War Diaries and Intelligence Summaries are contained in F. S. Regs., Part II. and the Staff Manual respectively. Title Pages will be prepared in manuscript.

Place	Date	Hour	Summary of Events and Information	Remarks and references to Appendices
In the field.	30/1/18		108th Inf. Bde. relieved 109th Inf. Bde. in line; 109th Bde. relieved 108th Bde. in DURY Area.	
"	31/1/18		Lines patrolled and tested.	

3/2/18

for [signature] Lieut
O.C., 36th Div. Sig. Coy., R.E.

SECRET

Army Form C. 2118.

Instructions regarding War Diaries and Intelligence Summaries are contained in F. S. Regs., Part II. and the Staff Manual respectively. Title pages will be prepared in manuscript.

WAR DIARY
or
INTELLIGENCE SUMMARY. 36th Divl.Sig.Coy.R.E.
(Erase heading not required.)

Vol 9

Place	Date	Hour	Summary of Events and Information	Remarks and references to Appendices
In the Field	1.2.18		Lines patrolled. Line laid from HAMEL LOCK to 108th M.G. Company.	
"	2.2.18		Lines patrolled, and old cable reeled up.	
"	3.2.18		Line repaired to O.P. 99.	
"	4.2.18		Nothing to report.	
"	5.2.18		Nothing to report.	
"	6.2.18		Building poled route from O.P.99 to CASTRES.	
"	7.2.18		Building poled route from O.P.99 to CASTRES, staking done where necessary.	
"	8.2.18		Lines laid from Batteries to O.P.99.	
"	9.2.18		Four Low poled route staked and poled from O.P.99 over CANAL, and work on buried cable routes.	
"	10.2.18		-do-	
"	11.2.18		Exchange at O.P.99 established, poled route over CANAL continued and staking three pairs over marsh towards GONTESCOURT. Work on buried cable routes.	
"	12.2.18		-do-	
"	13.2.18		Finished route and ran lines into GONTESCOURT Exchange.	
"	14.2.18		Lines completed from O.P.99 to RAPHAEL O.P. Work done on buried cable routes, also lines run into new Div.H.Q. Signal Office.	

2353 Wt. W3411/1454 700,000 5/15 D.D.&L. A.D.S.S/Forms/C. 2118.

SECRET

Army Form C. 2118.

WAR DIARY
or
~~INTELLIGENCE SUMMARY~~

(Erase heading not required.)

Instructions regarding War Diaries and Intelligence Summaries are contained in F. S. Regs., Part II. and the Staff Manual respectively. Title pages will be prepared in manuscript.

Place	Date	Hour	Summary of Events and Information	Remarks and references to Appendices
In the Field	15.2.18		109th Inf. Bde. relieved 107th Inf. Bde. in line at HAMEL LOCK.	
"	16.2.18		Line put through to GIFFICOURT Exchange by 109th Bde. section. Work on buried cable routes, and new Div. H.Q. Signal office.	
"	17.2.18		Picking up old cable and work on new Signal office.	
"	18.2.18		-do-	
"	19.2.18		Line put through from 109th M.G. Coy. to their right and left sections.	
"	20.2.18		109th Bde. Section Signal office transferred to a Cellar.	
"	20.2.18		Signal Sub-Section R.E. attached 153rd Bde. R.F.A. relieved by 148th Bde. Cable buried into new H.Q. GRAND SERAUCOURT by No.3 Section. New buried cable route from 109th Bde. Signal office to Battalion H.Q. Battle in QUARRY commenced.	
"	21.2.18		Line laid from M B test point to Right Battalion of 109th Bde. thence to RENE O.P. thus connecting Bde. H.Q. to RENE O.P. direct. Burying cable into new H.Q. GRAND SERAUCOURT by No.3 Section.	
"	22.2.18		Lines laid to Batteries. Burying cable into new H.Q. GRAND SERAUCOURT.	
"	23.2.18		No.3 Section moved in new Headquarters. Office opened 3 p.m.	
"	24.2.18		Overhauling equipment. Cables at new H.Q. Divl. Signal office,duplicated into cellar.	
"	25.2.18		-do-	
"	26.2.18		-do-	

SECRET

Army Form C. 2118.

WAR DIARY
or
INTELLIGENCE SUMMARY
(Erase heading not required.)

Instructions regarding War Diaries and Intelligence Summaries are contained in F. S. Regs., Part II. and the Staff Manual respectively. Title pages will be prepared in manuscript.

Place	Date	Hour	Summary of Events and Information	Remarks and references to Appendices
In the Field	27.2.18		Duplicating lines into cellar of new Div. Sig. H.Q. Signal office. General overhaul of equipment. Lamp and flag practices carried out.	
"	28.2.18		Lamp, Flag and Buzzer practices. Cable jointing lecture. Cleaning and overhauling cable carts and signal equipment.	

Brown
Capt.
for O.C., 36th Div. Sig. Coy., R.E.

36th Divisional Engineers

36th DIVISIONAL SIGNAL COMPANY R. E.

MARCH 1918

Army Form C. 2118.

36 D Signals
38th Div'l. Sig. Coy., R.E.
Vol 30

WAR DIARY
or
INTELLIGENCE SUMMARY
(Erase heading not required.)

Instructions regarding War Diaries and Intelligence Summaries are contained in F. S. Regs., Part II. and the Staff Manual respectively. Title pages will be prepared in manuscript.

Place	Date March 1918	Hour	Summary of Events and Information	Remarks and references to Appendices
OLLEZY	1st		Picking up Cable.	
"	2nd		Picking up Cable.	
"	3rd		Nothing to report.	
"	4th		Picking up Cable.	
"	5th		Nothing to report.	
"	6th		Nothing to report.	
"	7th		Picking up Cable.	
"	8th		Picking up Cable.	
"	9th		Nothing to report.	
"	10th		Nothing to report.	
"	11th		Working on Buried Routes forward & testing lines.	
"	12th		Picking up Cable.	
"	13th		Nothing to report.	
"	14th		Picking up Cable.	
"	15th		Working on Buried Routes forward and Testing Lines.	
"	16th		Working on Buried Routes forward and Testing Lines.	
"	17th		Working on Buried Routes forward and Testing Lines.	
"	18th		Working on Canniveu System.	
"	19th		Working on Canniveu System.	
"	20th		Working on Canniveu System.	

Army Form C. 2118.

WAR DIARY
or
INTELLIGENCE SUMMARY

38TH DIV. SIG. COY., R.E.

(Erase heading not required.)

Instructions regarding War Diaries and Intelligence Summaries are contained in F. S. Regs, Part II. and the Staff Manual respectively. Title Pages will be prepared in manuscript.

Place	Date	Hour	Summary of Events and Information	Remarks and references to Appendices
OLLEZY	March 21st		Heavy enemy bombardment opened at about 4.45 a.m. At 4.50 a.m. order was received to "Man Battle Stations".	
			At about 9 a.m. the main Buried Cable Route forward of GRAND SERAUCOURT was cut and a large party was sent out to mend it.	
			This severed all connections with the Right and Centre Battalions in the Forward Zone, though lines still held to the Left Battalion.	
			Owing to the very thick mist "visual" was impossible.	
			The carefully organized system of Wireless was useless owing to the fact that all the Forward Stations were either captured or badly gassed. The Divisional Wireless Officer was gassed on his way up to investigate the trouble.	
			Good Telephone communication was maintained with all Brigade Headquarters and the Artillery Groups throughout the day.	
			About 8 p.m. warning was received that Division Headquarters would move during the night to ESTOUILLY and all Brigade Headquarters and Artillery Brigade Headquarters to BRAY ST. CHRISTOPHE.	
			Lines were immediately started and laid direct between BRAY ST. CHRISTOPHE and ESTOUILLY	

Army Form C. 2118.

WAR DIARY
or
INTELLIGENCE SUMMARY

(Erase heading not required.)

36TH DIV. SIG. COY., R.E.

Place	Date	Hour	Summary of Events and Information	Remarks and references to Appendices
OLLEZY	21st		lateral and central lines from OLLEZY were laid to BRAY ST. CHRISTOPHE to connect up with the 61st Brigade who were by this time under this Division (10.30 p.m.) Signal Office opened ESTOUILLY 1 a.m. Closed OLLEZY 4 a.m.	
ESTOUILLY	22nd		About 3 p.m. warning was received that Division Headquarters would move to FRENISCHES and that Brigade Headquarters would move as follows :- 107th Brigade .... EAUCOURT 108th Brigade) 179th R.A.Bde.) ... BROUCHY. 109th Brigade) 61st Brigade .... VILLESELVE. During the afternoon Telephone lines were laid out accordingly. Opened Signal Office FRENISCHES 5 p.m. Closed Signal Office ESTOUILLY 6.30 p.m. During the night 22/23rd the Brigade Headquarters moved to their new Locations, but the 107th Brigade did not move to EAUCOURT and was located on the morning of the 23rd at CUGNY.	
	23rd		A line was put through on existing Permanent Route to EAUCOURT thereby connecting them with Division Headquarters (7 a.m.). Lines were maintained from FRENISCHES during the 23rd as follows :- All Infantry Brigades - 179 R.A. Brigade - 91st R.A. Brigade. Note :- The 153 rd Bde.	

Army Form C. 2118.

36TH DIV. SIG. COY., R.E.

WAR DIARY
or
INTELLIGENCE SUMMARY
(Erase heading not required.)

Instructions regarding War Diaries and Intelligence Summaries are contained in F. S. Regs., Part II. and the Staff Manual respectively. Title Pages will be prepared in manuscript.

Place	Date	Hour	Summary of Events and Information	Remarks and references to Appendices
ESTOUILLY	23rd. March 1918		had by this time joined the 30th Division R.A.	
			Division Headquarters moved during afternoon to BEAULIEU. Lines having previously being put through. An advanced Exchange and Report Centre was kept open in FRENISCHES.	
			During the night of 23rd all Brigades had moved :-	
			107th and 108th to BERLANCOURT. 109th and 61st to VILLESELVE. 153rd and 279th Brigades R.F.A. to FLAVY LE MELDUEX.	
	24th		All the above units were in Telephone communication with FRENISCHES during most of the 24th.	
			As the lines between FRENISCHES and BEAULIEU passed through LIBERMONT and ERCHEU it was thought advisable to lay two direct lines through FRETOY LE CHATEAU as the enemy had penetrated ESMERY - HALLON and threatened LIBERMONT.	
			About 5 p.m. the lines from FRENISCHES to BEAULIEU via LIBERMONT were disconnected and for a time there was no communication other than D.R. However at about 7 p.m. direct cables were put through via FRETOY + LE - CHATEAU. About this time the enemy commenced heavy shelling of GUISCARD and the main GUISCARD - FRENISCHES road and thereby broke all communication with the Infantry Brigades.	
			During the night 24th/25th Advanced Exchange was withdrawn from FRENISCHES.	

Army Form C. 2118

WAR DIARY
or
INTELLIGENCE SUMMARY

(Erase heading not required.)

36TH DIV. SIG. COY., R.E.

Instructions regarding War Diaries and Intelligence Summaries are contained in F.S. Regs., Part II. and the Staff Manual respectively. Title Pages will be prepared in manuscript.

Place	Date	Hour	Summary of Events and Information	Remarks and references to Appendices
	24th		The Infantry Brigades were concentrated in the BREAULIEU Area and placed under orders of the 62nd French Division. who took over the line.	
	25th.		Division Headquarters moved to AVRICOURT, by which time lines had been put through to BEAULIEU. Advanced Exchange was left open at BEAULIEU until the afternoon for the R.A. Headquarters who moved at about 4 p.m. The Division R.A. came under orders of the French and was detached from early morning of 25th keeping with it a complete Cable detachment. The 61st Brigade rejoined its own division. The whole Division received orders to concentrate in the WARSY BECQUIGNY area. Signal Office at AVRICOURT was handed over to the French. Division Headquarters moved in the afternoon tp CHATEAU at WARSY where Signal Office was opened on arrival (5 p.m.). All Brigade Headquarters moved to WARSY.	
	26th		Early on 26th information was received that there was a gap in the line between the British and the French and the Division was ordered to hold the line from ANDECHY to AVRE and Brigade Headquarters were disposed as follows :-	

1875. Wt. W593/826 1,000,000 4/15 J.B.C. & A. A.D.S.S./Forms/C. 2118.

Army Form C. 2118

36TH DIV. SIG. COY., R.E.

WAR DIARY
or
INTELLIGENCE SUMMARY

(Erase heading not required.)

Instructions regarding War Diaries and Intelligence Summaries are contained in F.S. Regs., Part II. and the Staff Manual respectively. Title Pages will be prepared in manuscript.

Place	Date	Hour	Summary of Events and Information	Remarks and references to Appendices
	March 1918 26th		107th Brigade Headquarters ... GUERBIGNY. 108th Brigade Headquarters ... ERCHES. 109th Brigade Headquarters ... On the GUERBIGNY & AND ERCHY road. Visual Signalling was established to all Brigades from high ground near WARSY and a Runners post established there. After dark the enemy was reported to have attacked our positions and a transmitting Visual Station was captured. Germans were reported entering GUERBIGNY and Division Headquarters moved to BECQUIGNY. Touch was maintained with Brigades by Runners and Motor Cyclists, but during the night two Motor Cycl sts were captured.	
	27th		Early in the morning of 27th Division Headquarters moved to FIGNIERES. At about 9 a.m. cable was laid out to WARSY to get touch with Brigades, but by the time it reached WARSY Brigade Headquarters had all left and enemy were attacking in force. In the afternoon Division Headquarters moved to HARGICOURT and a Signal Office was opened there. Later in the evening the Division was relieved by the 56th Division (French) and Division Headquarters moved to SOURDON where Signal Office was opened at 8 p.m. Brigades were ordered to concentrate in HARGICOURT Area.	

Army Form C. 2118.

WAR DIARY
or
INTELLIGENCE SUMMARY

36TH DIV. SIG. COY., R.E.

(Erase heading not required.)

Place	Date	Hour	Summary of Events and Information	Remarks and references to Appendices
	28th		Division put under orders of 166th French Division about 9 p.m. moved as follows :-	
			107th Brigade and 109th Brigade to COULLEMELLE and 108th Brigade to SOURDON.	
			During the night 28th/29th a line was put through partly cable partly French Permanent Route to an Advanced Divisional Report Centre at COULLEMELLE. Owing to French interference with the line linemen were out continually in order to keep it through.	
			Lines were laid to connect up 107th and 109th Brigades to Advanced Division Exchange	
	29th		Division Headquarters moved to WAILLY at 8 p.m. and Brigades moved to CHAUSSOY, EPAGNY and EPAGNY.	
	30th		Division entrained for GAMACHES where Signal Office was opened and Division Headquarters established at 9 p.m.	
	31st		Location Brigades on arrival :-	
			107th Brigade ... TULLY.	
			108th Brigade ... AULT.	
			109th Brigade ... FLUQUIERES.	

Muray
Capt.,
for O.C. 36th Div. Sig. Coy., R.E.

25th April, 1918.

36th Divisional Engineers

36th DIVISIONAL SIGNAL COMPANY R.E. :: APRIL 1918.

Secret.

36th DIV. SIG. COY., R.E.

Army Form C. 2118.

WAR DIARY
or
INTELLIGENCE SUMMARY

(Erase heading not required.)

Place	Date	Hour	Summary of Events and Information	Remarks and references to Appendices
GAMACHES	1/4/18		Division stationed at GAMACHES. Cleaning and overhauling Equipment. Division Artillery at ETOUY. 173rd Brigade R.F.A. at LA RUE ST. PIERRE.	
-do-	2/4/18		All equipment overhauled. Communication established with 109th Brigade through French Exchange. Division Artillery, 173rd and 163rd Brigades R.F.A. move to FRANCASTEL.	
-do-	3/4/18		Division left GAMACHES for FLEQUIÈRES where they entrained for PROVEN. 108th Brigade entrained at EU STATION at 9.15 pm, detrained at 12.15 pm on the 4/4/18 and moved to HERZEELE. 109th Brigade marched from TULLY to WOINCOURT where they entrained at 7 pm, detrained at ROUSBRUGGE (Belgium), and proceeded to BORDER CAMP. Communication established by telephone to Division via Second Corps. Division Artillery moved to MORVILLERS, 173rd Brigade R.F.A. Section moved to OFFIGNIES, and 163rd Brigade R.F.A. Section marched to MORVILLERS-ST-SATURIN.	

Secret.

33RD DIV. SIG. COY, R.E.

Army Form C. 2118.

WAR DIARY
~~INTELLIGENCE SUMMARY.~~

(Erase heading not required.)

Instructions regarding War Diaries and Intelligence Summaries are contained in F. S. Regs, Part II. and the Staff Manual respectively. Title pages will be prepared in manuscript.

Place	Date	Hour	Summary of Events and Information	Remarks and references to Appendices
GAMACHES	4/9/18		Line laid from Division Artillery to 173rd Brigade R.F.A. at OFFIGNIES. Stores and equipment examined and deficiency lists sent to O.C. Signals POIX collecting Area.	
POPERINGHE	5/9/18		Division detrained at PROVEN and marched to TEN ELMS CAMP	
- do -	6/9/18		109th Brigade moved into Divisional Support with H.Q. at CANAL BANK direct communication established to 1st and 2nd Royal Inniskilling Fusiliers. 9th Royal Inniskilling Fusiliers were under command of 107th Brigade in the line. 109th Brigade came under orders of 1st Division.	
- do -	7/9/18		Battle Zone reconnoitred by Runners and Linemen.	
CANAL BANK	8/9/18		Division left TEN ELMS CAMP for CANAL BANK to relieve 1st Division in the line. Division Artillery moved to MOYENCOURT. OFFIGNIE'S line reeled up before leaving. 153rd Brigade R.F.A. Signal Sub-Section moved to MOYENCOURT-SOUS-POIX. 173rd Brigade R.F.A. Signal Sub-Section moved to COURCELLES.	

Secret.   38TH DIV. SIG. COY., R.E.

3.

WAR DIARY
or
INTELLIGENCE SUMMARY

(Erase heading not required.)

Army Form C. 2118.

Place	Date	Hour	Summary of Events and Information	Remarks and references to Appendices
CANAL BANK	9/9/18		108th Brigade entrained at HERZEELE at 10 am, detrained at POPERINGHE and marched to HOSPITAL FARM, opening office at 3 pm.	
-do-	10/9/18		Main cable laid to EB Test point to pick up lines for Battle zone. 108th Brigade moved at 2 pm to KEMMEL, office opened at 6 pm.	
-do-	11/9/18		Advance Party of 108th Brigade moved to WULVERGHEM, thence to KEMMEL HILL. Divisional Artillery and 113th Brigade R.F.A. moved to PONT DE NIEPPE, 153rd Brigade Signal Section marched to RENANCOURT	
-do-	12/9/18		Cable cart collecting cable. 109th Brigade moved from CANAL BANK to ALBERTA, relieving the 107th Brigade, 1st and 2nd Royal Inniskilling Fusiliers in the line. Divisional Artillery on to 3rd Corps office at SALEUX by means of old French Routes.	
-do-	13/9/18		Visual established between ALBERTA and RACECOURSE FARM Runner routes established to each Battalion.	

Secret.

Army Form C. 2118.

36TH DIV. SIG. COY., R.E.

WAR DIARY
or
INTELLIGENCE SUMMARY

(Erase heading not required.)

Place	Date	Hour	Summary of Events and Information	Remarks and references to Appendices
CANAL BANK	14/4/18		Arrangements made for distribution of Test Points in the event of a withdrawal.	
			108th Brigade Headquarters moved to HUBNER FME.	
			Divisional Artillery, 153rd and 173rd Brigades R.F.A., D.A.C. and (C. 1 Company) Divisional Train entrained at ST. ROCHE (AMIENS) for HOPOUTRE and POPERINGHE.	
-do-	15/4/18		109th Brigade moved from ALBERTA to CANAL BANK prior to withdrawal from the line.	
			Divisional Artillery detrained at HOPOUTRE and marched to MONASTERY MONT-DES-CATS. From on to 9th Corps. 153rd Brigade R.F.A. L/L Section detrained at HOPOUTRE Siding POPERINGHE and bivouacked near GODEWAERSVELDE.	
-do-	16/4/18		108th Brigade H.Q. moved to LA CLYTTE. Battalions moved to CLYDESDALE Plain.	
			Cable laid to R.H. test point.	
			153rd Brigade R.F.A. Section went into action near BERTHEN under 32nd Division.	
			Artillery Visual & telephone communication established.	

Secret.

Army Form C. 2118.

38TH DIV. SIG. COY., R.E. 5

WAR DIARY
or
INTELLIGENCE SUMMARY.
(Erase heading not required.)

Place	Date	Hour	Summary of Events and Information	Remarks and references to Appendices
CANAL BANK	17/9/18		Commenced setting up channel cable to CANAL BANK and forward areas.	
			Runner post established at IRISH FARM. As result of enemy shelling the 107th Brigade H.Q. was moved from LA CLYTTE to rear of village, communication being maintained by runner to Battalions 107th Brigade H.Q moved to HOSPITAL FARM.	
			113rd Division Artillery moved to ST SILVESTRE CAPELLE, m.t. 9.R. to/o Kings Park. 113rd Brigade RFA went into action over BERTHEN under 36th Division Artillery	
-do-	18/9/18		Work on advising cable continued. RA HQ section less 2 telephonists moved to BOESCHEPE to assist 38th Div Artillery.	
-do-	19/9/18		Work on advising cable continued. R.A. Section working on line from 143rd Brigade RFA to advanced 38th Division Artillery at MONT NOIR. Line continually being broken by shell fire.	
-do-	20/9/18		Work on advising cable continued.	

Secret.

38TH DIV. SIG. COY. R.E. WAR DIARY or INTELLIGENCE SUMMARY.

Army Form C. 2118.

(Erase heading not required.)

Instructions regarding War Diaries and Intelligence Summaries are contained in F.S. Regs., Part II. and the Staff Manual respectively. Title pages will be prepared in manuscript.

Place	Date	Hour	Summary of Events and Information	Remarks and references to Appendices
CANAL BANK	21/9/18		Work on being cable continued. Brigade HQ moved along CANAL BANK to position erected by Divisional Headquarters	
BORDER CAMP	22/9/18		Division left CANAL BANK for BORDER CAMP. 38th Advanced Division closed at MONT NOIR	
POPERINGHE	23/9/18		R.A. Section R.F.A. rejoined Division. Artillery at St SILVESTRE, 153rd Brigade R.F.A. Section came out of action and marched to HAMHOEK, east of POPERINGHE and rejoined Division.	
—do—	24/9/18		Division Artillery moved to TEN ELMS CAMP. On to 2nd Corps, 153rd and 173rd Brigades R.F.A, 173rd Brigade came out of action and moved to HAMHOEK.	
—do—	25/9/18		Reeling up cable 153rd and 173rd Brigades R.F.A. Sections moved to BRIELEN, both on to sgn. H.A.C at TROIS TOURS	

Secret.

Army Form C. 2118.

36TH DIV. SIG. COY., R.E.

WAR DIARY
or
INTELLIGENCE SUMMARY
(Erase heading not required.)

Instructions regarding War Diaries and Intelligence Summaries are contained in F. S. Regs., Part II, and the Staff Manual respectively. Title pages will be prepared in manuscript.

Place	Date	Hour	Summary of Events and Information	Remarks and references to Appendices
POPERINGHE	2/4/18		Picking up cable.	
			Divisional Artillery reported Division at BORDER CAMP and took over from 66th Division	
			Artillery at 5 pm, 153rd Brigade R.F.A. came into Action and took over from 330th Brigade	
			(66th Division) on CANAL BANK, 173rd Bde. R.F.A moved to SIEGE CAMP A. to 36th Division.	
do	3/4/18		Office closed BORDER CAMP at 11 am and opened at DRAGON CAMP, 107th Brigade	
			HQ moved from HOSPITAL FARM to A.26.b.5.6. advanced station near WINDMILL on POPERINGHE	
			ELVERDINGHE ROAD, 36th Divisional Signal School under Lieut. Brewer R.E. entrained at	
			TROIS ROIS (PROVEN), detrained at DOLLEZEELE, and proceeded to MILLIAM.	
			Divisional Artillery moved with Division to DRAGON CAMP at 11 am, leaving	
			advanced Exchange at BORDER CAMP till lines forward disconnected as one of the Corps test	
			points and no records available 173rd Brigade R.F.A moved to HOSPITAL FARM. Rear	
			of 153rd Brigade R.F.A. Section continually being broken by shell fire.	
			Horses, Transport and Q.M. stores moved to X Camp.	

Secret.

36TH DIV. SIG. COY., R.E.

WAR DIARY or INTELLIGENCE SUMMARY

Army Form C. 2118.

Place	Date	Hour	Summary of Events and Information	Remarks and references to Appendices
POPERINGHE	28/9/18		Picking up cable and patrolling lines. Visual established between Battalions and 108th Brigade Headquarters. Advanced Division Artillery closed at BORDER CAMP at 7 pm. 173rd Brigade moved to CANAL BANK into action. 3 pairs forward to 153rd and 173rd Brigades R.F.A.	
-do-	29/9/18		Reeling up cable. Horses, Transport and Q.M. stores moved to LA LOVIE CHATEAU	
-do-	30/9/18		Reeling up cable.	

A. Mahieu Capt.
for O.C. 36th Div Sig Coy R.E.

SECRET.

Army Form C. 2118.

38TH DIV. SIG. COY., R.E. "WAR" DIARY

or

~~INTELLIGENCE SUMMARY.~~

(Erase heading not required.)

Instructions regarding War Diaries and Intelligence Summaries are contained in F. S. Regs., Part II. and the Staff Manual respectively. Title pages will be prepared in manuscript.

Place	Date MAY.	Hour	Summary of Events and Information	Remarks and references to Appendices
In the Field	1st		Headquarters at DRAGON CAMP. Horse lines at LOVIE. Old cables reeled up, lines patrolled and tested. 109th Brigade at CANAL BANK.	
"	2nd		107th Brigade at CANAL BANK. Salving Cable and overhauling Equipment.	
"	3rd		Salving Cable.	
"	4th		Repairing and patrolling Lines. Salving Cable.	
"	5th		Salving Cable.	
"	6th		Test Points taken over and Lines tested.	
"	7th		Nothing to report.	
"	8th		Capt. A.H. Bishop, M.C., R.E. joined from 34th Divisional Signal Company, R.E.	
"	9th		Work on Staked Cable Routes forward.	
"	10th		Capt. H.A.M. Napier, A.& S.H. proceeded to 33rd Divl. Sig. Coy., R.E 109th Brigade took over front of Left Brigade. 41st Division being relieved by 107th Brigade. Lines fixed up for new positions of Battalions.	
"	11th		Lines put through for Battalion at GLOSTER.	
"	12th		S.H. Test Point which had been destroyed, partially repaired and lines put through. New line laid to Brigade O.P. (109th Brigade)	
"	13th		Lines patrolled.	

Army Form C. 2118.

36TH DIV. SIG. COY., R.E. WAR DIARY

or ~~INTELLIGENCE SUMMARY~~

(Erase heading not required.)

Instructions regarding War Diaries and Intelligence Summaries are contained in F. S. Regs., Part II. and the Staff Manual respectively. Title pages will be prepared in manuscript.

Place	Date MAY	Hour	Summary of Events and Information	Remarks and references to Appendices
In the Field	14th		Lines patrolled.	
	15th		Repairing Lines.	
	16th		Lines picked up at English Farm.	
	17th		107th Brigade relieved by 108th Brigade.	
	18th		Relief complete 3.0 a.m.	
	19th		Work on Staked Cable routes. Practice with Flag and lamp.	
	20th		Ditto.	
	21st		Work on Staked Cable Routes.	
	22nd		- Do -	
	23rd		- do -	
	24th		DAHALLOW. New line laid by 109th Brigade to Advanced Dressing Station at	
	25th		Cable salved and repaired.	
	26th		Patrolling lines.	
	27th		Cable salved and patrolling lines.	
	28th		Lines ran to Brigade H.Q. near STEENTJE. New line laid to Amplifier Station at CNB.	
	29th		107th Brigade relieved 108th Brigade in the Line	

Army Form C. 2118.

36TH DIV. SIG. COY., R.E. WAR DIARY or ~~INTELLIGENCE SUMMARY~~.

(Erase heading not required.)

Instructions regarding War Diaries and Intelligence Summaries are contained in F. S. Regs., Part II. and the Staff Manual respectively. Title pages will be prepared in manuscript.

Place	Date	Hour	Summary of Events and Information	Remarks and references to Appendices
In the Field.	MAY 30th		Salving and repairing Cable.	
	31st		- do -	

B. Bonner Capt.,
for O.C. 36th Divl. Sig. Coy., R.E.

46/18

Army Form C. 2118.

WAR DIARY
or
INTELLIGENCE SUMMARY.

(Erase heading not required.)

36th Divl Signal Coy. R.E.

SECRET

Instructions regarding War Diaries and Intelligence Summaries are contained in F.S. Regs., Part II. and the Staff Manual respectively. Title pages will be prepared in manuscript.

Place	Date JUNE	Hour	Summary of Events and Information	Remarks and references to Appendices
In the Field	1st	......	Patrolling lines.	
- do -	2nd	......	- do -	
- do -	3rd	......	Nothing to report	
- do -	4th	......	- do -	
- do -	5th	......	Moved from DRAGON CAMP to PARDO CAMP (Proven) on relief by BELGIAN DIVN.	
- do -	6th	......	Overhauling equipment.	
- do -	7th	......	- do -	
- do -	8th to 20th	......	Carried out training in Visual Signalling (Flag, Lamp & Helio) Infantry drill Gas drill, Physical drill & Range practice.	
- do -	21st	......	109th Bde Signals moved to REYNOLDS CAMP (Proven) and took over Billets and Signal Office from 107th Bde Signals, communications established at 11 a.m. Billets and Signalling Office at TUNNELLING CAMP taken over by Signals 107th Bde.	
- do -	22nd to 29th	......	Continued Training.	
- do -	30th	......	Signals 107th Bde Signals moved to CORNETTE and Signals 109 Bde to TUNNELLING CAMP. 108th Bde moved from CORNETTE to PROVEN Area. Divisional Signal School located at RUBROUCK.	

4/7/18

[signature]
Capt..
for O.C. 36th Divl. Sig.Coy., R.E.

Army Form C. 2118.

SECRET.

WAR DIARY
or
INTELLIGENCE SUMMARY.
(Erase heading not required.)

Instructions regarding War Diaries and Intelligence Summaries are contained in F. S. Regs., Part II. and the Staff Manual respectively. Title pages will be prepared in manuscript.

36th SIGNAL COMPANY — *36th DIVISION*
No. .... Date ....

Vol 34

Place	Date	Hour	Summary of Events and Information	Remarks and references to Appendices
PARDO CAMP (PROVEN)	1	.....	Divisional Horse Show held at PROVEN	
DO	2	.....	Nothing to Report	
DO	3	.....	Moved from PARDO CAMP to CASSEL. Office closed at COUTHOVE CHATEAU and opened at CASSEL at 10 a.m.	
CASSEL	4	.....	Continued training - Visual Signalling, Flag, Lamp, Helio, etc.	
DO	5	.....	do	
DO	6	.....	do	
DO	7	.....	Divisional Advanced H.Q. moved to MONT-Des-CATS. Brigades moved forward from CASSEL, area to ST JAN'S CAPPEL Sector and relieved French Division in the line. Lieut. A.R. McClure, H.L.I., joined from 2nd Army Signal Coy., R.E.	
MONT-Des-CATS	8	.....	Lines put through to new positions. Fullerphones installed	
do	9	.....	Rear H.Q. moved from CASSEL to TERDEGHEM. Laying and testing lines. Old French lines overhauled.	
DO	10	.....	Laying and testing lines	
DO	11	.....	do.	
DO	12	.....	Reeling up old cable	
DO	13	.....	Lecture on Signalling to Aeroplanes	
DO	14	.....	Divisional Advanced H.Q. moved to KEKKEM TERDEGHEM. 109th Brigade moved to CONVENT, MONT-DesnCATS (Reserve Brigade Headquarters).	

Army Form C. 2118.

WAR DIARY
or
INTELLIGENCE SUMMARY
(Erase heading not required.)

Instructions regarding War Diaries and Intelligence Summaries are contained in F. S. Regs., Part II and the Staff Manual respectively. Title pages will be prepared in manuscript.

Place	Date	Hour	Summary of Events and Information	Remarks and references to Appendices
TERDEGHEM	July 15		Lieut. A. T. Terry, R.E., left for 56th Divl. Signal Coy., R.E. Salving Cable.	
DO	16		2/Lieut. M. Duncan, R.F.A., reported from Xth Corps Signals for duty. Reeling up old cable.	
DO	17		Reeling up old cable.	
DO	18		Nothing to report	
DO	19		Lieut. V.H. Gately, M.G. Corps, taken on strength 19.7.18 for duty with No. 5 Section.	
DO	20		Work on burying cable	
DO	21		Lieut. H.E. Blake, "The Buffs", joined from Xth Corps Signals. Work on buried cable forward of MONT-Des-CATS	
DO	22		Testing visual communications. Burying Cable.	Testing message carrying rockets
DO	23		Patrolling and testing lines. Burying Cable.	
DO	24		Salving old cable. Burying Cable	
DO	25		Communication carried out by Wireless and Visual between 6 a.m. and 8 p.m.	
DO	26		Work on buried cable.	
DO	27		do	
DO	28		do	
DO	29		11th Course at the 36th Divisional Signal School dispersed at RUBROUCK.	

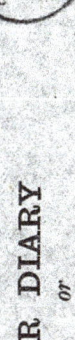

Army Form C. 2118.

WAR DIARY
or
INTELLIGENCE SUMMARY
(Erase heading not required.)

36TH SIGNAL COMPANY — 36th DIVISION

Instructions regarding War Diaries and Intelligence Summaries are contained in F. S. Regs., Part II. and the Staff Manual respectively. Title pages will be prepared in manuscript.

Place	Date	Hour	Summary of Events and Information	Remarks and references to Appendices
TERDEGHEM	July 30		Work on buried Cable. Overhauling and cleaning equipment.	
DO	31		Work on buried Cable. Preparing wagons and teams for 2nd Army Signals Horseshow.	

[signature] Capt.,
for O.C. 36th Div. Signal Coy., R.E.

Army Form C. 2118.

WAR DIARY
INTELLIGENCE SUMMARY
(Erase heading not required.)

36TH DIV. SIG. COY., R.E.

Aug.

Place	Date	Hour	Summary of Events and Information	Remarks and references to Appendices
TERDEGHEM	1918 Aug. 1		Routine. Cable overhauled.	
	2		A good deal of work was done repairing lines to Brigades which had been cut	
	3		Considerable enemy activity/causing trouble in maintaining lines. Work was done on buries. Artillery	
	4		Company paraded at Church to commemorate Anniversary of the commencement of the war.	
	5		Routine. Work on buries. Inspection of Cable Wagons and Horse Lines. Lecture by Genl. Maxse.	
	6		Inspection by H.M. King George and presentation of Medals at OXELEARE.	
	7		Routine. Lecture by General Maxse.	
	8		108th Brigade relieved by 109th Brigade in Line. Considerable trouble with lines in BERTHEN Area.	
	9		Routine. Enemy's Artillery very active on positions on which our linemen were working	
	10		Routine. Our detachments working on buries in SCHAEXEN and BERTHEN area were delayed considerably owing to activity of enemy's Artillery fire.	
	11		Special Parade Service at TERDEGHEM at which the King attended. March Past.	
	12		Routine. Inspection of Cable detachments and Horse Lines.	
	13		Routine. Work on buries continued.	
	14		do.	
	15		do.	
	16		do.	
	17		do. Inspection and Recreational Training.	

Army Form C. 2118.

WAR DIARY
or
INTELLIGENCE SUMMARY.
(Erase heading not required.)

Instructions regarding War Diaries and Intelligence Summaries are contained in F. S. Regs., Part II. and the Staff Manual respectively. Title pages will be prepared in manuscript.

Place	Date	Hour	Summary of Events and Information	Remarks and references to Appendices
XXXXXXXXXX TERDEGHEM.	Aug. 18		Routine. Work on buried systems hampered somewhat owing to enemy's artillery.	
	19		Routine. Inspection of Horses and Wagon Lines. Work on buries continued.	
	20		Quiet day. Lines patrolled and improvements made.	
	21		Routine. Work on buries.	
	22		A successful attack was made and the line advanced. Enemy's counter attack unsuccessful. The work on the buries was continued. Inspection of horses.	
	23		Considerable enemy activity. The buried systems were connected to Brigade Signal Stations. Artillery	
	24		Attack was made; objectives captured. Enemy's Artillery very active causing dislocation of communication for a time.	
	25		Quiet day. Routine inspection.	
	26		do.	
	27		ST JANS CAPPEL was heavily shelled. Maintenance of lines.	
	28		Nothing of particular interest to report. Cable on hand was overhauled and tested.	
	29		Routine. Maintenance of buries.	
	30		BAILLEUL evacuated by the enemy. Enemy retiring. 108th Brigade moved to MONT Des CATS. Order for relief by 31st Division cancelled.	
	31		Advance continued. MT KEMMEL captured. 107th Brigade moved to MT KOKEREELE. Lines laid and maintained throughout day. 108th Brigade moved to St JANS CAPPEL area. Communication established. Advanced Divisional Headquarters was opened at MONT Des CATS at 8 a.m.	

[signed] Capt.
O.C., 36th Div. Sig. Coy. R.E.

Army Form C. 2118.

WAR DIARY
or
INTELLIGENCE SUMMARY. 36TH DIV. SIG. COY., R.E.

(Erase heading not required.)

Instructions regarding War Diaries and Intelligence Summaries are contained in F.S. Regs., Part II. and the Staff Manual respectively. Title pages will be prepared in manuscript.

Place	Date	Hour	Summary of Events and Information	Remarks and references to Appendices
September	1		Advanced Div. H.Q. at MONT Des CATS. Rear Divisional H.Q. at TERDEGHEM. Advanced H.Q. moved to ST JANS CAPPEL. Rear HQ. moved to ST SYLVESTRE CAPPEL. 107th Brigade moved to MT KOKEREELE, 108th Brigade moved to TRESCAULT HOUSE, 109th Brigade moved to neighbourhood of RAVELSBURG. Lines to Brigades and Advance Exchange opened at BAILLEUL ASYLUM. Enemy retiring. 108th Brigade moved to MT NOIR. Lines laid in touch with all Brigades and flank Divisions.	Ref. Maps 28.S.W.1 Trench Maps.
	2		Enemy continues retiring. Rear Div. HQ closed 7.50 a.m. ST SYLVESTRE CAPPEL, opened ECKE same time. 7.30 p.m. 107th Brigade moved to BAILLEUL ASYLUM. 108th Brigade moved to S.18.a.5.7. Lines continued.	
	3		108th Brigade moved to T.19.b.9.8. Line continued to them. Line laid out to 29th Division at T.17.b.1.6. Line laid to 107th Brigade in vicinity of NEUVE EGLISE from Advanced Exchange in NEUVE EGLISE.	
	4		Much damage done to lines by hostile shelling. Maintenance carried on throughout the day. Heavy Gas Shelling. In touch with flank Divisions, 29th on right and 30th on our left.	
	5		Considerable difficulty in maintaining lines owing to heavy hostile Gas Shelling. Enemy counter attack. 107th Brigade relieved 108th Brigade. 108th Brigade opened at BAILLEUL ASYLUM 8.10 p.m. 31st Division relieved 29th Division on our right.	
	6th		Advanced Division report centre opened FIX EXCHANGE on the RAVELSBERG RIDGE. Attack launched by 107th Brigade. Maintenance of lines was carried out during the day. Advanced Report Centre closed and returned to ST JANS CAPPEL 7.40 p.m.	
	7th		General improvement of the system of important communications carried out. Very bad weather and considerable difficulty experienced in locating earth faults.	
	8th		108th Brigade moved to rest at MONT Des CATS. Line laid and Visual Communication established. 109th Brigade in reserve at S.18.a.5.7.	
	9th		Visual stations to Brigade reconnoitred. Maintenance Maintenance and localisation of faults carried out during the day.	

Army Form C. 2118.

WAR DIARY
or
INTELLIGENCE SUMMARY.
(Erase heading not required.)

Instructions regarding War Diaries and Intelligence Summaries are contained in F. S. Regs., Part II. and the Staff Manual respectively. Title pages will be prepared in manuscript.

(2).

Place	Date	Hour	Summary of Events and Information	Remarks and references to Appendices
September				
	10th		Visual Station manned and practise messages sent. Men were rested and bathed. Kit Inspection.	
	11th		Maintenance of line to Brigade carried out. Much damage to lines owing to hostile shelling	
	12th		Work on buries. Locating old buried systems.	
	13th		Continued work on old buries. Old routes were tested, faults located and lines put through.	
	14th		Maintenance of lines. Routine. A good deal of the spare time spent in Gas Drill.	
	15th		107th Brigade in line relieved by 109th Brigade. 107th Brigade moved to BERTHEN. 109th Brigade moved into support, Headquarters at S.18.a.5.7. Lines laid to 107th Brigade.	
	16th		Routine. Maintenance and improvement of lines. Visual communication to 107th Brigade established.	
	17th		Advanced Exchange at NEUVE EGLISE heavily shelled.	
	18th		Routine.	
	19th		Warning Order that Division would move into rest received.	
	20th		Linemen sent to ESDAILE Camp. Preparations for move.	
	21st		Rear and Advanced HQ. closed 11 a.m. and opened ESDAILE Camp same time. 107th Brigade moved to WORMHOUDT Area. Headquarters at ESQUELBECQUE, 108th Brigade moved to STEENVOORDE, 109th moved to EECKE. Communications through Corps Exchange.	
	22nd		109th Brigade moved to WORMHOUDT.	
	23rd		Inspections. Cable overhauled and repaired.	
	24th		Work on Brigade lines. Cable Wagons inspected. Inspection of Horse Lines.	

WAR DIARY
or
INTELLIGENCE SUMMARY. 36th DIV. ENG. COY., R.E.

(3).

(Erase heading not required.)

Army Form C. 2118.

Instructions regarding War Diaries and Intelligence Summaries are contained in F. S. Regs., Part II. and the Staff Manual respectively. Title pages will be prepared in manuscript.

Place	Date	Hour	Summary of Events and Information	Remarks and references to Appendices
September	25th		Routine. Inspections &c. Nothing of special interest to report.	
	26th		108th Brigade moved from HOUTEKERQUE to ROAD CAMP. 109th " " " WORMHOUDT to SCHOOL CAMP 107th " " " ESQUELBECQUE to TUNNELLING CAMP. Capt. Macdonald arrived.	
	27th		107th Bde. moved to BROWN CAMP. Line laid to them. 109th " " " DIRTY BUCKET CAMP. Line to them through Corps. Div. HQ. closed ESDAILE CAMP 4 p.m. Opened VOGELTJE CHATEAU same time.	
	28th		Big attack commenced. 109th Brigade moved to REIGERSBURG CHATEAU. Communication to them by Corps buries. 108th Bde. moved to area west of YPRES. 107th Bde. moved to POTIZE. Line laid to them at 3.30 p.m. Div. HQ. closed VOGELTJE 2 p.m., opened Ramparts YPRES same time. Wagon lines moved to position W of BIRR CROSS ROADS. Casualties, 5 killed and 19 wounded (caused by shell landing on cable detachment coming through YPRES). Communication established with 9th Division on left and 29th Division on right. 108th and 109th Brigades moved in night to POLYGON BUTTS. 2nd Corps laid lines to our Advanced Exchange at CLAPHAM JUNCTION	
	29th		Attack launched by 109th Bde. with 108th Bde. in support. Line laid to POLYGON BUTTS, via GHULEVELT at 11 a.m. from Advanced Exchange. Considerable difficulty owing to hostile shelling and bad state of country in maintaining this line. Alternate pairs laid from Advanced Exchange via XXXXXXX WESTHOEK TERHAND captured.	
	30th		Div. HQ. moved to BACELEARE 7 a.m. Line extended from CLAPHAM JUNCTION.	

Army Form C. 2118.

WAR DIARY
or
INTELLIGENCE SUMMARY.

(Erase heading not required.)

36th Divisional Signal Coy., R.E.

Vol 37

Place	Date	Hour	Summary of Events and Information	Remarks and references to Appendices
October	1st		Wagon Lines moved to BECELEARE. CLAPHAM JUNCTION closed. Rear Headquarters moved to JUNCTION CAMP, ST JEAN. Lines to them extended through Corps buries. 109th Bde. moved to PEASE CORNER. Maintenance of Lines. Working Morse to Corps Headquarters.	
	2nd		Heavy hostile shelling on horse lines. 5 horses wounded. Lieut Moss slightly wounded. Horse Lines moved to REUTEL.	
	3rd		108th Bde. relieves 107th Bde. 109th Bde. at DADIZEELE.	
	4th		Quiet day. Inspection of men. Gas Helmet Drill.	
	5th		Situation unchanged. General improvement of lines. Inspection of horses and wagons.	
	6th		107th Bde. moved to POLYGON BUTTS. Lines laid.	
	7th		Adv. Div HQ. returned to JUNCTION CAMP, ST JEAN, leaving Report Centre, behind at BECELEARE. 109th Bde. moved to DIRTY BUCKET CAMP. Communication to them through 2nd Corps.	
	8th		Quiet day. Cable thoroughly overhauled and repaired. Reinforcements arrived, inspected and posted to Sections.	
	9th		Situation unchanged.	
	10th		Two lines laid to GUINESS FARM. Advanced Division returned to KILT FARM.	
	11th		107th Bde. moved to GUINESS HOUSE. 109th Bde. moved to BASS FARM. A third pair was laid to GUINESS FARM, one line for Infantry, one for Artillery and an alternative to be used by either.	
	12th		Attack commenced 5.35 a.m. Forward positions for lines reconnoitred. Two O.K. to ASHMORE FARM.	
	13th		Attack proceeding. Advanced Division moved to ASHMORE FARM 9 a.m. 107th and 109th Bdes. moved to SILVER FARM. Two lines laid to Corps Advance at DADIZEELE. Lines continued by Cable Detachments to SILVER FARM. Earth line laid to BARLEY CORNER not used by Brigades. Rear HQ closed at JUNCTION CAMP and opened at KILT FARM. 108th Bde. moved to ASHMORE FARM and on to SHILLING FARM.	

Army Form C. 2118.

WAR DIARY
or
INTELLIGENCE SUMMARY.

36th Divisional Signal Coy., R.E.

(*Erase heading not required.*)

Instructions regarding War Diaries and Intelligence Summaries are contained in F. S. Regs., Part II. and the Staff Manual respectively. Title pages will be prepared in manuscript.

Place	Date	Hour	Summary of Events and Information	Remarks and references to Appendices
October	15th		Attack proceeding. Considerable difficulty in maintaining the lines. The cable detachments were out most of the day and night repairing breaks. 108th Bde. moved to ASHMORE FM.	
	16th		Orders re relief by 41st Division received. Considerable difficulty in maintaining communication to Brigades. Advanced Division closed at ASHMORE FM. 1700, opened SPARK FM. same time.	
	17th		Rear HQ. closed at KILT FM. E.2a2 0110. Moved to SPARK FM. Lines laid to 107th Brigade at ROLEGHEMCAPPELLE, 108th Bde. at DRIE MASTEN, 109th Bde at LEDEGHEM. D.R.L. Lorry destroyed by fire.	
	18th		Adv. Div. HQ opened at LENDELEDE 1500. Line laid to Advance from Corps Adv. Headquarters at WINKLE ST ELOI. D5 single laid to 3rd BELGIAN DIVI. Line laid to Brigades at VULGERY FM.	
	19th		107th and 109th Bdes moved to B17 Central near HULSTE. Line laid to them. Advanced Exchange opened at Bde HQ.	
	20th		107th Bde. moved to C 20.c. near OYGHEM. Line laid to them. 108th Bde. moved to B.17 Central Line from SPARK FM. to LENDELEDE reeled up. All cable in vicinity of SPARK FM. salved.	
	21st		Advanced Exchange opened at C.20.8. 109th Bde. opened at C.20.c. Inspection of men and Baths parade.	
	22nd		Routine. Improvement of lines.	
	23rd		All horse transport moved to C.3.b. near DRIES.	
	24th		Advanced Div HQ opened at C.3.b. near DRIES at 1100. 108th Bde. moved to 14.d.4.5. Pair laid to DEERLYCK to meet Corps pair. 107th Bde. relieved by 109th Bde.	

Army Form C. 2118.

WAR DIARY
or
INTELLIGENCE SUMMARY.
36th Divisional Signal Coy., R.E. (3).

(Erase heading not required.)

Place	Date	Hour	Summary of Events and Information	Remarks and references to Appendices
October	25th		109th Bde. moved to KLIJTBERG. Line extended to them. Pair laid to French Division near OOSTROOSEBEKE.	
	26th		107th Bde. moved to LENDELEDE. Warning order for relief received. Officer from 34th Division arrived and shown run of lines. Quiet day.	
	27th		Arrangements for move completed. 107th Bde. moved to BEIIEGHEM.	
	28th		Division moved to BEIIEGHEM. Came under 10th Corps. Line laid to 107th Brigade.	
	29th		108th and 109th Brigade moved to HULSTE.	
	30th		108th Brigade moved to LAUWE. Line laid. 109th Brigade moved to ST - ANNE. Line laid. Routine. Inspection and Baths.	
	31st		Inspection of Wagons and horses.	

Capt.,
for O.C.36th Divisional Signal Coy., R.E.

36TH DIV. SIG. COY., R.E.

WAR DIARY
or
INTELLIGENCE SUMMARY

NOVEMBER 1918

Army Form C. 2118.

Vol 36

Place	Date	Hour	Summary of Events and Information	Remarks and references to Appendices
BELLEGHEM	29.10.18		Routine. Lines run to 109 Bde at ST ANNE and to 108 Bde at LAUWE. Three surplus pennants were handed to 102 Field Coy R.E. Three ton lorry broken down and beyond local repair, at COURTRAI.	
do	30.10.18		Reduplicating line to 108 Bde & relaying signal line. Shopochon of cable carts & waggons. Routine baths, recreational training etc. Court of enquiry into the loss of the belongings to 57822 Sergt. (K)ccisy, 109 Bde. Checking & overhauling stores.	
do	31.10.18		Routine. 109 Bde	
do	1.xi.18		107 Bde moved to RECKEM. Laid line to 107 Bde new position from 108 Bde at LAUWE.	
do	2.xi.18		Routine	
do	3.xi.18		107 and 108 Bdes moved to MOUSCRON area. Sent 5 men & 1 (local) stores to open office there with 14th Div. Laid lines from 14th Div to 107 and 108 Bdes. Corps laid one line to me.	

WAR DIARY or INTELLIGENCE SUMMARY.

(Erase heading not required.)

36th DIV. SIG. COY., R.E.

Army Form C. 2118.

Place	Date	Hour	Summary of Events and Information	Remarks and references to Appendices
MOUSCRON	4.XI.18		Headquarters opened at MOUSCRON at 11 am. Laid line from ROLLEGHEM to MOUSCRON for lateral to 30th DIVN. at BELLEGHEM.	
do	5.XI.18		Routine. Laid line to 5 M.A.C.	
do	6.XI.18		Routine	
do	7.XI.18		Routine	
do	8.XI.18		Routine & Recreational Training	
do	9.XI.18		do	
do	10.XI.18		do	
do	11.XI.18		Routine & Recreational Training. Hostilities ceased at 11 am	
do	12.XI.18		do	
do	13.XI.18		do. Came under X Corps	
do	14.XI.18		do	
do	15.XI.18		109 Mble moved to RONCQ. Line to them via X Corps	

36TH DIV. SIG. COY., R.E.

Army Form C. 2118.

WAR DIARY
or
INTELLIGENCE SUMMARY.
(Erase heading not required)

Instructions regarding War Diaries and Intelligence Summaries are contained in F. S. Regs., Part II. and the Staff Manual respectively. Title pages will be prepared in manuscript.

Place	Date	Hour	Summary of Events and Information	Remarks and references to Appendices
MOUSCRON	16.xi.18		Routine.	
do	17.xi.18		Parade at ROUBAIX.	
do	18.xi.18		⎫	
do	19.xi.18		⎬ Routine	
do	20.xi.18		⎭	
do	21.xi.18			
do	22.xi.18		Routine. Transferred to XV Corps at 1200	
do	23.xi.18		⎫	
do	24.xi.18		⎬	
do	25.xi.18		⎬ Routine	
do	26.xi.18		⎬	
do	27.xi.18		⎬	
do	28.xi.18		⎬	
do	29.xi.18		⎬	
do	30.xi.18		⎭	

MacDonald Capt.
O.C. 36th Division Signal Co.

WAR DIARY

36th DIV. SIG. COY., R.E.

INTELLIGENCE SUMMARY.

Army Form C. 2118.

Place	Date	Hour	Summary of Events and Information	Remarks and references to Appendices
MOUSCRON	Dec. 1		Church parade	
	2		Routine and recreational training	
	3		do	
	4		do	
	5		Moved from billets in Rue Theatre, Rue de Tourcoing to billets in Rue de Leopold	
	6		Routine and recreational training	
	7		do	
	8		Routine. Church parades	
	9		Overhauling unit equipment	
	10		do	
	11		Cleaning wagons and harness	
	12		Company paraded 0830 and marched to HALLUIN to take part in ceremonial parade	
	13		Routine, Education and recreational training	
	14		do	
	15		Church parades	
	16		Routine, Education and recreational training	
	17		do	
	18		do	
	19		do	
	20		do	

Army Form C. 2118.

WAR DIARY
38th DIV. SIG. COY., R.E.
or
INTELLIGENCE SUMMARY.

(Erase heading not required.)

Place	Date	Hour	Summary of Events and Information	Remarks and references to Appendices
MOUSCRON	Dec 21		Horse Transport moved to new billet in Rue de Courtrai	
	22		Church parades	
	23		Routine. Educational and Recreational Training	
	24		do	
	25		Routine and celebration of Xmas festivities	
	26		Routine	
	27		do Educational and Recreational Training	
	28		do Church parades	
	29		Horse Inspection. Church parades	
	30		Routine, Educational and recreational Training	
	31		do	

[signature]
O.C., 38th Div. Sig. Coy., R.E.

Army Form C. 2118.

WAR DIARY
of
INTELLIGENCE SUMMARY.
(Erase heading not required.)

JANUARY 1919.

36 D Signals Vol 40

Instructions regarding War Diaries and Intelligence Summaries are contained in F. S. Regs., Part II. and the Staff Manual respectively. Title pages will be prepared in manuscript.

Place	Date	Hour	Summary of Events and Information	Remarks and references to Appendices
MOUSCRON	JAN 1		Routine, Education & Recreational training.	
	2		do	
	3		Inspection of horses.	
	4		Church parades	
	5		Routine & Education	
	6		do	
	7		do Lecture by A.D.M.S.	
	8		Major C.H. Macmillan R.E. M.A. Capt A.H. Bishop MC RE assumed command.	
	9		Capt A.H. Bishop MC RE left for England district 7 strength Routine recreational training. Lecture by Professor T. Leccombe on League of Nations. Democracy. Dance for men of Coy.	
	10		Education & routine.	
	11		do	
	12		Church parades.	
	13		Routine Education. Lecture by Mr Packfield on Japanese life.	
	14		do & Cable Salvage	
	15		do do	
	16		do do	
	17		do Lectures by Mr Williams the Rev W.K. Greenland	
	18		Routine Education & Recreational training. Night class signal duties.	
	19		Church parades.	

WAR DIARY
or
INTELLIGENCE SUMMARY.
(Erase heading not required.)

Army Form C. 2118.

Place	Date	Hour	Summary of Events and Information	Remarks and references to Appendices
MOUSCRON	JAN. 20		Routine Education, cable salvage	
	21		do	
	22		do	
	23		do	
	24		do	
	25		do	
	26		Church parade	
	27		Routine Education, recreational training, cable salvage	
	28		do	
	29		do	
	30		do	
	31		Sergt J Mitchem attached C.S.M. to the company. Routine education, cable salvage